MODERN
20 Bold & Graphic Quilts
MINIMAL

ALISSA HAIGHT CARLTON

stashBOOKS®

an imprint of C&T Publishing

Publisher: Amy Marson

Creative Director: Gailen Runge

Acquisitions Editor: Susanne Woods

Editor: Liz Aneloski

Technical Editors: Mary E. Flynn, Gailen Runge, and Teresa Stroin

Cover/Book Designer: Kristy Zacharias

Production Coordinator: Jessica Jenkins

Production Editor: Alice Mace Nakanishi

Illustrator: Tim Manibusan

Flat Quilt Photography by Christina Carty-Francis and Diane Pedersen of C&T Publishing, Inc., unless otherwise noted; Style Photography by Bethany Nauert, unless otherwise noted

Published by Stash Books, an imprint of C&T Publishing, Inc., P.O. Box 1456, Lafayette, CA 94549

Library of Congress Cataloging-in-Publication Data

Carlton, Alissa Haight, 1976-

  Modern minimal : 20 bold & graphic quilts / Alissa Haight Carlton.

    p. cm.

  ISBN 978-1-60705-486-3 (soft cover)

  1. Patchwork--Patterns. 2. Quilting--Patterns. I. Title.

  TT835.C374137 2012

  746.46--dc23

                    2011026416

Printed in China

10 9 8 7 6 5 4 3

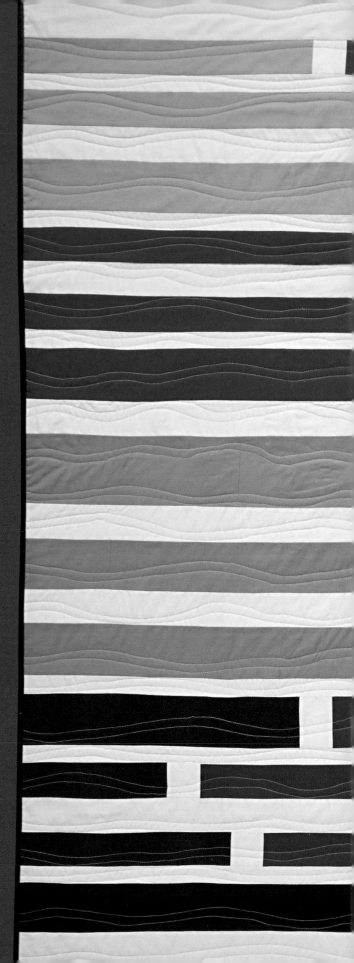

CONTENTS

Acknowledgments

There are so many people to thank!

First, my husband, Gavin, for all of his help through the months spent working on this book. He's always so supportive, and he's my first and last sounding board. I trust his taste and feedback completely, and I would be a weaker quilter (and person!) without him. I can always rely on him for support and love.

Thank you to Cate, my twin sister, who is the best friend I could have! Thank you to my parents for their constant encouragement.

To all of my quilting friends—both my friends at the Los Angeles Modern Quilt Guild and my online/blogging friends. The sense of community you've all given me has been immeasurably wonderful, so thank you!

Thanks to everyone who was so involved in making this book happen:

To folks at C&T Publishing—especially Susanne, Liz, Mary, Diane, and Kristy—for supporting me so much as an author and quilter.

Thank you to Janome for the wonderful Horizon Memory Craft 7700 sewing machine, Robert Kaufman Fabrics for providing the beautiful solid Kona cotton fabrics, and The Warm Company for its Warm and Natural batting.

A special thank-you to Bethany Nauert for her beautiful, inspiring style photography (bethanynauert.com).

Finally, a huge thank-you to Lori Lober, Terri Reyes, Harriet Zaretsky, Bill and Annie Macomber, and my lovely sister, Catherine Haight, for opening up their amazing homes for the style photography in this book. Their beautiful spaces made the quilts shine.

INTRODUCTION

About the Quilts in This Book

The patterns in this book are different from most quilt patterns you see. These designs were conceived by imagining the quilt top as a whole and ignoring the traditional idea that a quilt top needs to be made up of a grid of assembled blocks. This means that with just a few yards of some afford-able solid fabrics, the patterns sew up into beautiful, bold, graphic quilts. Some of these quilt tops can even be cut and sewn in one or two sittings, doing away with the idea that it takes ages to make a quilt.

Also appealing to many new or beginning quilters is that basic ¼"-seam piecing with straight lines is the focus of these patterns. There is not one finicky triangle or circle to be found in any of these quilts.

Because these quilts are minimal, there is a lot of open, negative space. The quilting adds quite a lot to the design, texture, and finished look of each quilt. As a result, for each pattern, I've offered two ideas of how to quilt the quilt. I hope you'll mix and match the ideas—or come up with entirely new quilting ideas of your own!

My overall approach and philosophy to quilting is that it can be done in a relaxed and fun way. I don't agree with the idea that you have to be a per-fectionist to be a great quilter. Although you need to pay close attention to craftsmanship, so that the quilt stays in good shape over the years, you don't need to be finicky and fussy. The patterns in this book all lend them-selves to that idea—so dive in and make a quilt or two! Don't be scared of mistakes or have a goal of "perfection." Perfect is boring; there's much more interest and beauty in the small discrepancies of each handmade quilt.

When making a quilt, most of us are not trying to win prize ribbons; we're just trying to make an attractive, functional quilt that we, our family, or our friends will get to snuggle under. This goal is accomplished even if a quilt comes out an inch shorter than planned. So don't sweat the small stuff. The more quilts you make, the more you'll really understand the ins and outs of each step and the better you'll get at it—so get sewing!

Notes on Making the Quilts in This Book

Since these quilts are not built block by block, I have some specific thoughts on making them that should help you.

Because a lot of the measurements in this book are longer than 42" (the standard measurement used as the width of fabric, or WOF), you are often instructed to sew together pieces of the same fabric to create one larger piece for the quilt top. This creates more seams in your quilt top, but it saves a lot of fabric and money and creates less waste. I also like the rustic and warm touch it gives these otherwise graphic designs.

Another thing that saves yardage is not being concerned with always keeping the straight grain of the fabric going the same direction. While some quilters might disagree with this idea, it works for me. In all the quilts I have made, I have usually switched the direction of the grain of my fabric, and doing so has never caused a problem for me. The usual argument against this technique is that it changes the drape of the fabric, which is absolutely true for garment sewing. But when quilts are finished they are densely quilted, and quilting affects the drape far more than the direction in which you cut the fabric. Therefore, when it saves fabric, I switch between cutting across the grain or with the grain.

For these patterns, I always added a quarter-yard to the needed quantities of each fabric. The fabric amounts are based on 42"-wide fabric, from selvage to selvage. Most quilting cottons are wider than that, but should prewashing shrink your fabrics, you'll still have enough. Also, the extra quarter-yard allows for a little wiggle room if you make a cutting error.

Lastly, the quilts are made of almost entirely solid fabrics, which gives them a wonderfully open, clean, and sophisticated look. However, sewing solids presents one small issue: There is no right side or wrong side to the fabric. As a result, when putting together your quilt top, it's sometimes easy to mistakenly sew to the wrong side of the piecing. Before sewing a seam, be sure to check the already completed seams to be certain that your seam allowances are all on the same side.

WHITE NEGATIVE SPACE

DRIP | 60" × 75"

CUTTING

Fabric A (orange)

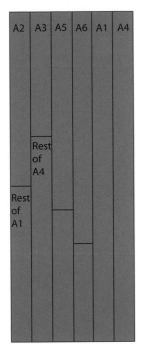

1. Cut 6 strips 2½" × WOF (width of fabric).

2. From 4 of the strips, cut A2, A3, A5, and A6.

3. Use the leftovers from cutting pieces A2 and A3. Piece each end to end to one of the 2 remaining whole strips. Cut A1 and A4.

    A1: 2½" × 53½"

    A2: 2½" × 21½"

    A3: 2½" × 15½"

    A4: 2½" × 45½"

    A5: 2½" × 24½"

    A6: 2½" × 28½"

TIP

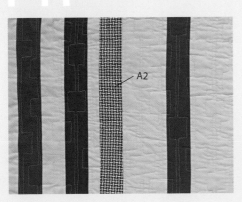

Why not throw in a monochromatic patterned fabric, as I've done with piece A2? I repeat this monochromatic pop of patterned fabric in a few quilts in this book. I think it is a great way to make a quilt pattern or design more uniquely your own.

This simple, bold modern lap quilt will add a pop of color to any living room. Why not make it as a wedding gift for the next cool couple you know getting married?

As with many of the projects in this book, cutting and piecing long strips is the focus here. This quilt top comes together very quickly.

Be careful when cutting the background fabric. It's probably the most challenging step. But if you follow the directions with care, you will have no problems!

WHAT YOU NEED

Based on 42" fabric width.

Fabric A (orange): ¾ yard

Fabric B (blue): ⅜ yard

Fabric C (gray): ¾ yard

Fabric D (ivory): 3½ yards for background

Backing: 4¼ yards

Binding: ⅞ yard

Please be sure to read Notes on Making the Quilts in This Book (page 6).

Fabric B (blue)

1. Cut 2 strips 2½" × WOF.

2. Piece the strips together end to end; cut B1.

    B1: 2½" × 57½"

Fabric C (gray)

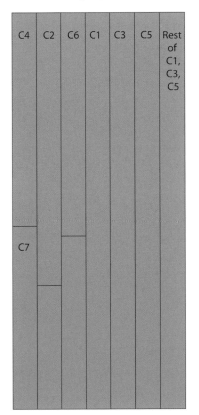

1. Cut 7 strips 2½" × WOF.

2. Cut C4 and C7 from a strip from Step 1.

3. Cut C2 and C6 from 2 of the strips from Step 1.

4. Piece the 4 remaining strips together end to end; cut C1, C3, and C5.

C1: 2½" × 48½"	**C4:** 2½" × 21½"	**C7:** 2½" × 18½"
C2: 2½" × 27½"	**C5:** 2½" × 42½"	
C3: 2½" × 60½"	**C6:** 2½" × 22½"	

As you cut out pieces, pin little labels on them so you can easily keep track of everything.

11

Cutting, continued

Fabric D (ivory)

The background pieces need to be cut exactly as instructed. It might look tough to tackle, but it's easy when you carefully think it through before cutting. Read through the instructions thoroughly before cutting.

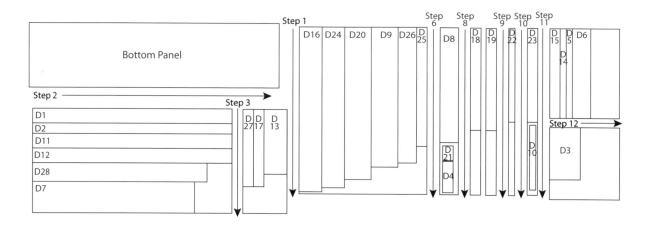

1. Cut 60½" × WOF from the full 3½-yard piece. Set aside the remainder of the fabric.

2. Working with the 60½" piece, cut a 60½" × 15½" piece for the bottom panel. Label and set aside.

3. From the rest of the 60½"-long fabric (now measuring 26½" × 60½"), cut a 26½" × 11½" piece. Set aside the remaining 49" × 26½" piece.

4. From the 26½" × 11½" piece, cut D13, D17, and D27.

5. From the 49" × 26½" piece, cut D1, D2, D7, D11, D12, and D28.

6. From the remaining portion of the original 3½-yard piece, cut 1 piece 31" wide × WOF.

7. Cut D9, D16, D20, D24, D25, and D26.

8. From the remainder of the original 3½-yard piece, cut 1 strip 4½" × WOF. Cut D4, D8, and D21.

9. Working with the remainder of the fabric, cut 2 strips 2½" × WOF and trim to make D18 and D19.

10. Cut 1 strip 1½" × WOF and trim to make D22.

11. Cut 1 strip 2½" × WOF and trim to make D23. With the remaining scrap, cut D10.

12. From the remaining original yardage, cut 21½" parallel to the selvage and cut D5, D6, D14, and D15.

13. Cut D3 from the last bit of the remaining original yardage.

Bottom panel: 60½″ × 15½″

D1: 3½″ × 48½″

D2: 2½″ × 48½″

D3: 7½″ × 12½″

D4: 2½″ × 7½″

D5: 1½″ × 21½″

D6: 4½″ × 21½″

D7: 7½″ × 39½″

D8: 4½″ × 27½″

D9: 6½″ × 33½″

D10: 1½″ × 15½″

D11: 3½″ × 45½″

D12: 3½″ × 45½″

D13: 5½″ × 15½″

D14: 1½″ × 21½″

D15: 2½″ × 21½″

D16: 5½″ × 39½″

D17: 2½″ × 18½″

D18: 2½″ × 24½″

D19: 2½″ × 24½″

D20: 6½″ × 36½″

D21: 2½″ × 3½″

D22: 1½″ × 22½″

D23: 2½″ × 22½″

D24: 5½″ × 38½″

D25: 2½″ × 28½″

D26: 4½″ × 32½″

D27: 2½″ × 18½″

D28: 4½″ × 42½″

Assembling the Quilt Top

Press after each step.

Assemble as shown in the quilt assembly diagram. Be sure to sew the background fabric onto the correct edge of the drip fabric, since it is different from drip to drip.

Making the Quilt Back

To make a 70″ × 84″ quilt back, cut 2 pieces 70″ × WOF and remove the selvages. Sew the 2 pieces together along the 70″ edges.

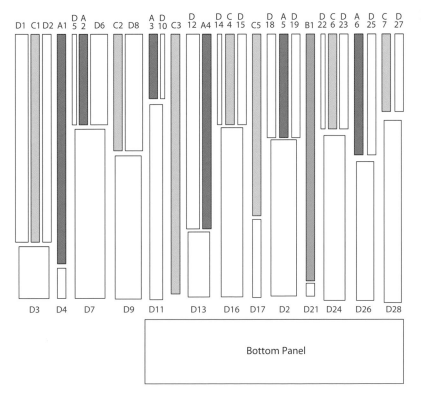

Quilting Options

OPTION 1

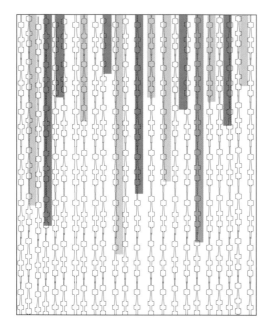

OPTION 2

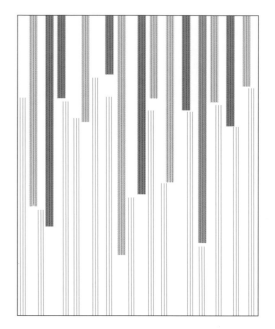

I quilted with a "mod" boxy pattern that I created with my free-motion foot. To make this pattern, I worked in lines from the top to the bottom of the quilt. The lines mirror each other, creating the box look. When I started a new row of boxes, I offset them so that they nested between the boxes from the previous row.

I started in the center of the quilt and worked to the right. Once I finished the first half, I rotated the quilt 180° and started in the middle again, working my way to the right again to fill in the whole quilt. See a close-up of the actual quilting (page 137).

Another option is to quilt a simple straight-line pattern that accentuates the vertical drips. The lines coming up from below in an asymmetrical fashion also add interest.

To do this, start in the middle and work your way to the right. When you want to end a line, backstitch 1 or 2 stitches (or use a locking stitch if your machine has one), lift the presser foot, and adjust so the continued line to the bottom end of the quilt is offset. Make sure you sew these locking stitches so that you can go back and trim all the running quilting threads and none of your quilting will come unsewn.

Once you've worked your way all the way to the right of the quilt, rotate the quilt 180°. Again, start in the middle and work your way to the right.

TIP

The drips create a guide to keep your quilting lines straight at the top of the quilt, but using masking tape as a straight edge can help too.

15

Graphic and hip, this quilt would be loved by any recipient. A twin-size quilt, it is perfect as a large throw over a daybed or for a single bed.

This is the only quilt in the book that is pieced with a border. Borders are incredibly common in traditional quilting patterns, but I rarely use them in my designs. Even in this quilt, there is a border in the construction, but it reads as an extended background rather than as a defined separate border.

WHAT YOU NEED

Based on 42" fabric width.

Fabric A (gray): ½ yard

Fabric B (black): 1 yard

Fabric C (blue): 6" × 15½"

Fabric D (ivory): 5 yards

Backing: 5 yards

Binding: ⅞ yard

Please be sure to read Notes on Making the Quilts in This Book (page 6). Label the pieces as you cut.

CUTTING

The color pops in the quilt are referred to as "bars." All bars are 15½" long, but their width varies. The gray, black, and blue fabrics will be used to make the bars and are framed in background fabric before being trimmed to the correct width.

Fabric A (gray)

1. Cut 1 strip 15½" wide.

2. Cut the strip into 3 strips:

15½" × 19½"
15½" × 9½"
15½" × 7"

Fabric B (black)

1. Cut 2 strips 15½" × WOF (selvage to selvage).

2. Cut the first strip to 15½" × 32½".

3. Cut the second strip twice:

15½" × 18"
15½" × 14½"

Fabric C (blue)

This strip is already cut to size.

Fabric D (ivory)

Cutting out the background fabric is a bit more involved than the bars but is straightforward if you just do it step by step.

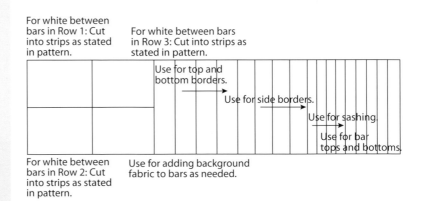

For white between bars in Row 1: Cut into strips as stated in pattern.

For white between bars in Row 3: Cut into strips as stated in pattern.

Use for top and bottom borders.

Use for side borders.

Use for sashing.

Use for bar tops and bottoms.

For white between bars in Row 2: Cut into strips as stated in pattern.

Use for adding background fabric to bars as needed.

ROWS 1-3 VERTICAL STRIPS

1. First cut: Cut a piece 28″ wide × WOF. Set aside the remaining fabric.

2. Second cut: Cut in half, parallel to the selvages. Trim the 2 pieces 28″ wide carefully to 20½″ high.

3. Cut 1 piece (for Row 1) to:

    D1: 4 strips 1½″ × 20½″

    D2: 3 strips 2½″ × 20½″

    D3: 4 strips 3½″ × 20½″

4. Cut the other piece (for Row 2) to:

    D4: 6 strips 1½″ × 20½″

    D5: 2 strips 2½″ × 20½″

    D6: 4 strips 3½″ × 20½″

5. Third cut: Cut a piece 26″ × WOF. Set aside the remaining fabric.

6. Fourth cut: Trim a piece 26″ wide × 20½″ high for Row 3.

7. Cut the piece for Row 3 to:

    D7: 6 strips 1½″ × 20½″

    D8: 4 strips 2½″ × 20½″

    D9: 2 strips 3½″ × 20½″

BAR TOP AND BOTTOM BACKGROUND

1. Cut 6 strips 4½″ × WOF (D10).

2. Cut 1 strip 5½″ × WOF (D11).

BORDERS

1. Cut 4 strips 9″ × WOF for the top and bottom borders.

2. Sew the strips in pairs end to end to make 2 long strips 9″ wide; trim each to 65½″.

3. Cut 4 strips 7½″ × WOF for the side borders.

4. Sew the strips in pairs end to end to make 2 long strips 7½″ wide; trim each to 67½″.

SASHING

1. Cut 4 strips 4″ × WOF.

2. Sew the strips in pairs end to end to make 2 long strips 4″ wide; trim each to 51½″.

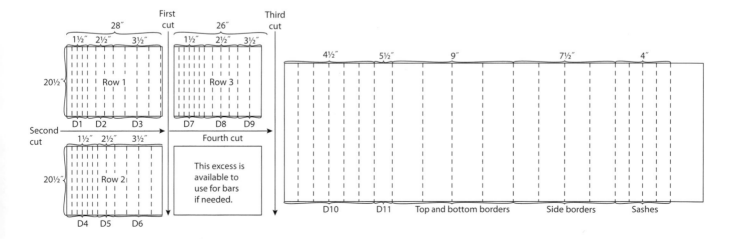

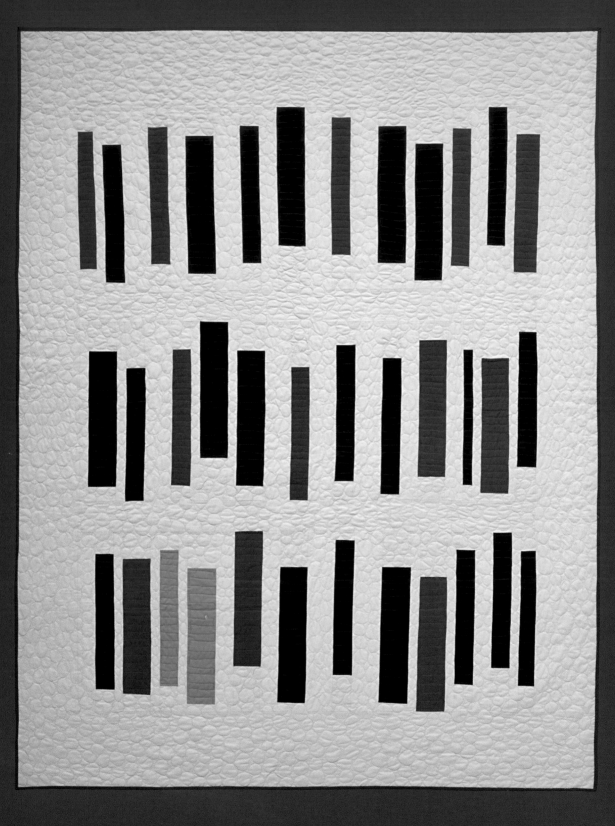

Assembling the Quilt Top

Press after each step.

MAKING THE BAR ROWS

All bars are 15″ high (finished). The "opposite sides" referred to in the following instructions could also be seen as the top and bottom.

1. Sew a D10 onto opposite sides of the 6″ × 15½″ blue bar piece; trim off the excess D10 strips. Press. Cut into the following 2 pieced components:

C1: 2½″ wide

C2: 3½″ wide

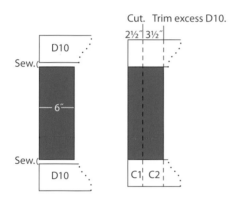

2. Sew a D10 onto opposite sides of the 32½″ × 15½″ black bar piece; trim off the excess D10 strips. Press. Cut into the following 11 pieced components:

B1: 2½″ wide   **B11:** 3½″ wide

B2: 3½″ wide   **B12:** 2½″ wide

B3: 2½″ wide   **B13:** 2½″ wide

B5: 3½″ wide   **B14:** 1½″ wide

B6: 3½″ wide   **B15:** 3½″ wide

B8: 3½″ wide

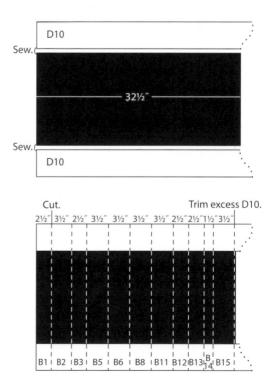

3. Sew a D10 onto opposite sides of the 18″ × 15½″ black bar piece. Trim off the excess D10 strips. Press. Cut the following 6 pieced components:

B16: 2½″ wide   B19: 3½″ wide

B17: 3½″ wide   B20: 2½″ wide

B18: 2½″ wide   B22: 3½″ wide

4. Sew a D10 onto opposite sides of the 19½″ × 15½″ gray bar piece. Trim off the excess D10 strips. Press. Cut the following 7 pieced components:

A1: 2½″ wide   A5: 3½″ wide

A2: 2½″ wide   A6: 2½″ wide

A3: 2½″ wide   A8: 3½″ wide

A4: 2½″ wide

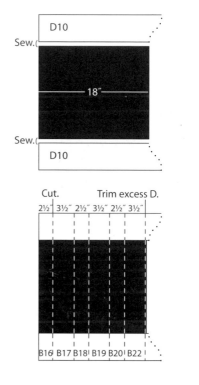

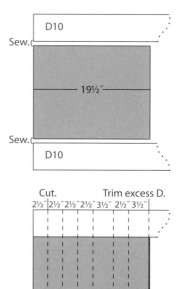

5. Sew a D10 onto opposite sides of the 7″ × 15½″ gray bar piece. Trim off the excess D10 strips. Press. Cut the following 2 pieced components:

A9: 3½″ × 15½″

A10: 3½″ × 15½″

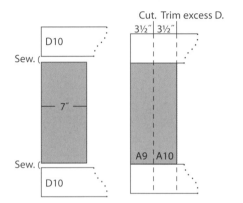

6. Sew a D11 onto only one side of the remaining gray bar piece. Trim off the excess D11 strip. Press. Cut the following 3 pieced components:

A7: 2½″ × 15½″

A11: 3½″ × 15½″

A12: 3½″ × 15½″

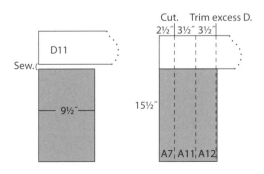

7. Sew a D11 onto only one side of the remaining black bar piece. Trim off the excess D11 strip. Press. Cut the following 5 pieced components:

B4: 3½″ wide

B7: 2½″ wide

B9: 2½″ wide

B10: 3½″ wide

B21: 2½″ wide

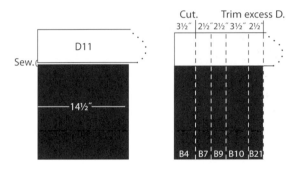

8. Working with bars A1, A5, B12, B16, and B20, trim the white background ends on both ends to 2¾″. Each bar will measure 20½″ long.

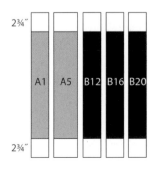

9. Working with A2, A4, A6, A8, B2, B5, B8, B11, B14, B22, and C1, trim the white background on the top end to 2¼″ and trim the white background on the bottom end to 3¼″. When you place the bars into their respective rows, turn bars A6, B2, B8, B11, and B14 upside down. Each bar will measure 20½″ long.

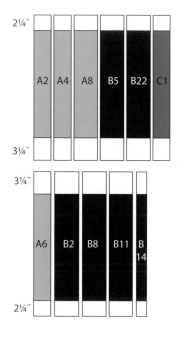

10. Working with A3, B1, B3, B6, B13, B15, B17, B18, B19, and C2, trim the white background on the top end to 1¼″. When you place the bars into their respective rows, turn bars B1, B6, B13, B17, B19, and C2 upside down. Each bar will measure 20½″ long.

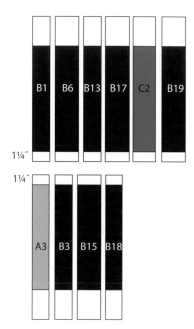

22

11. Next, working row by row and from left to right, use the bars and the Fabric D background strips and piece together Rows 1, 2, and 3. Press. It is important to keep a uniform seam allowance during this process so that the rows all end up the same length. Carefully reference the assembly diagram (below) to make sure that you're piecing everything in the correct order and using the correct widths of background fabric between the bars.

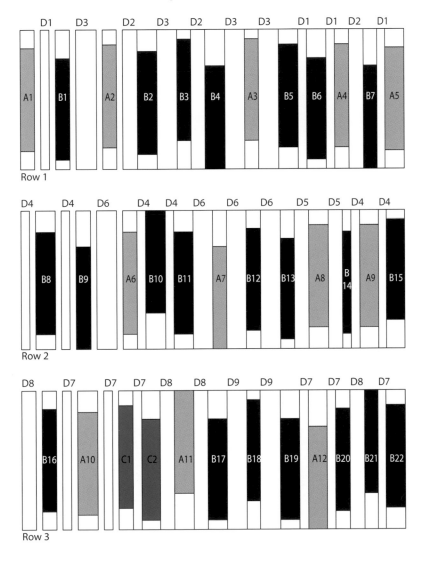

ADDING SASHING AND BORDERS

1. Sew the 3 rows to the 2 sashing strips and press.

2. Add the side borders and press.

3. Add the top and bottom borders and press.

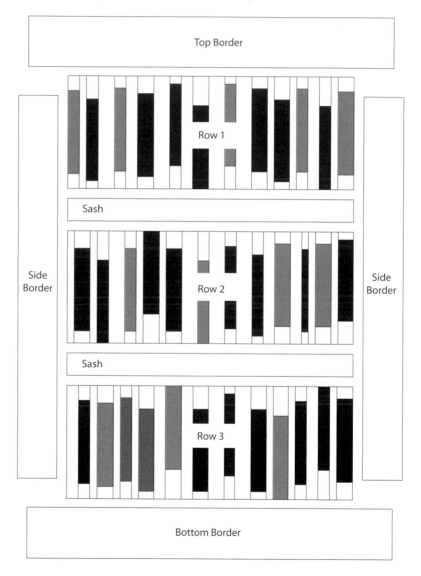

Making the Quilt Back

To make a 75″ × 94″ quilt back, cut 2 pieces 75″ × WOF and remove the selvages. Sew the 2 pieces together along the 75″ edges. Then add 10″ more to the bottom as follows: Cut 2 strips 10½″ × WOF, piece them together end to end, trim to 75″, and sew the long strip to the bottom of the quilt back.

Quilting Options

OPTION 1

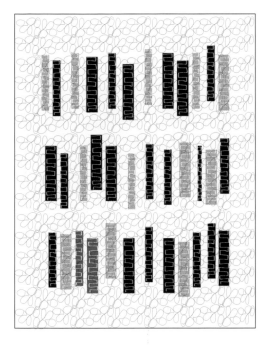

OPTION 2

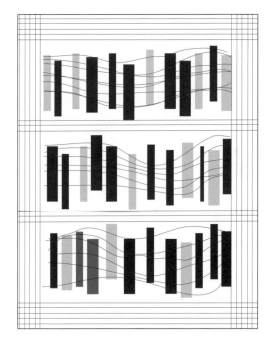

I created a lot of texture on this quilt by doing 2 different types of free-motion quilting. First, I stitched a straight-line rectangular pattern to fill in all the bars. Then, I worked my way around the quilt top, filling in all the open space with pebble quilting.

Another way to quilt this would be to first sew dense wavy lines that mirror the wave layout created by the bars. Do this all over the 3 rows of bars. Then, add some dense straight lines between the rows and over the top and bottom borders. Finish quilting by sewing more dense straight lines on the right and left borders of the quilt.

BROKEN STRIPES | 70″ × 80″

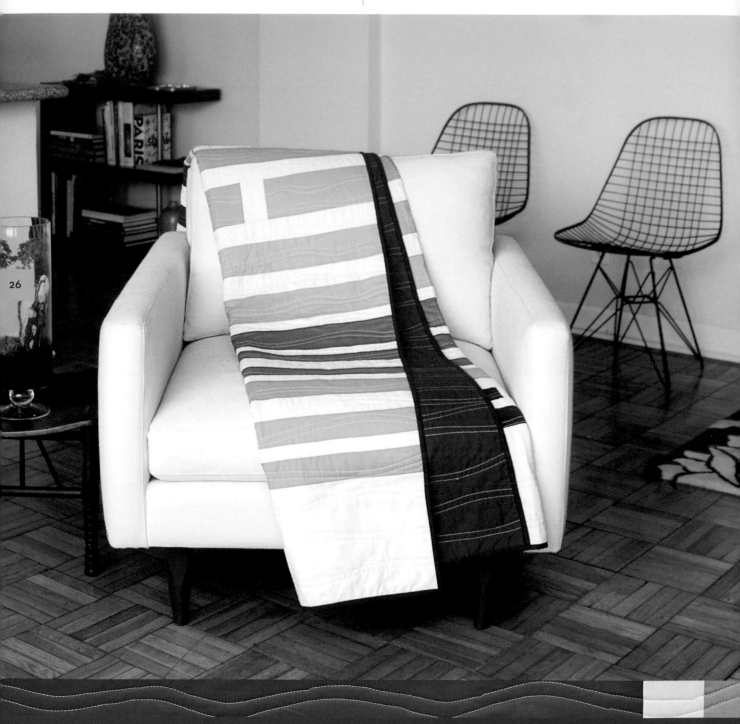

CUTTING

For this quilt top, you have to cut, piece, and then cut up the piecing. Then piece some more. As a result, the cutting and piecing instructions are combined.

Fabric A (gold)

1. Cut 1 strip 8½" × WOF (width of fabric); trim to 8½" × 30½" (A1).

2. Cut 1 strip 11½" × WOF; trim to 11½" × 26½" (A2).

Fabric B (brick red)

Cut 2 strips 8½" × WOF and sew together end to end; trim to 8½" × 48½" (B1) and 8½" × 20½" (B2).

Fabric C (teal blue)

1. Cut 4 strips 8½" × WOF.

2. Sew pairs of strips together end to end into 2 long strips; trim to 8½" × 48½" (C1) and 8½" × 56½" (C2).

Fabric D (tan)

Cut 1 strip 8½" × WOF; trim to 8½" × 30½" (D1).

Fabric E (lime green)

1. Cut 2 strips 11½" × WOF; sew end to end and trim to 11½" × 58½" (E1).

2. Cut 1 strip 8½" × WOF.

3. Trim the leftover piece from Step 1 to 8½" wide and add it to the end of the 8½" × WOF strip. Trim to 8½" × 43½" (E2).

Fabric F (chocolate brown)

Cut 1 strip 8½" × WOF; trim to 8½" × 40½" (F1).

This striped throw would be a great addition to any room. The horizontal stripes give you so many options to make the quilt your own through new and different color choices and combinations.

This quilt is pieced in sections, using a strip-piecing technique that makes cutting and piecing the strips simple. Strip piecing is not usually done on this large a scale, but the principle of piecing strips, cutting them, and then piecing more is the same.

WHAT YOU NEED

Fabric A (gold): ⅞ yard

Fabric B (brick red): ¾ yard

Fabric C (teal blue): 1¼ yards

Fabric D (tan): ½ yard

Fabric E (lime green): 1¼ yards

Fabric F (chocolate brown): ½ yard

Fabric G (cream): 3¼ yards for background

Backing: 5¼ yards

Binding: ⅞ yard

Please be sure to read Notes on Making the Quilts in This Book (page 6). Label the pieces as you cut.

Fabric G (cream)

1. Cut the background fabric pieces that separate the "stripes" in each section:

4 strips 2½" × 8½"

1 strip 2½" × 11½"

2. Cut the strips for between the stripes:

14 strips 1½" × WOF

14 strips 2½" × WOF; sew the strips together in same-width pairs and trim to 70"

3. Cut the strips for the top and bottom panels:

2 strips 9½" × WOF; sew end to end and trim to 9½" × 70" (bottom panel)

2 strips 12½" × WOF; sew end to end and trim to 12½" × 70" (top panel)

SECTION 1

Fabric A1: 8½" × 30½"

Fabric B1: 8½" × 48½"

Background fabric: 8½" × 2½"

SECTION 2

Fabric C1: 8½" × 48½"

Fabric D1: 8½" × 30½"

Background fabric: 8½" × 2½"

SECTION 3

Fabric E1: 11½" × 58½"

Fabric A2: 11½" × 26½"

Background fabric: 11½" × 2½"

SECTION 4

Fabric B2: 8½" × 20½"

Fabric C2: 8½" × 56½"

Background fabric: 8½" × 2½"

SECTION 5

Fabric F1: 8½" × 40½"

Fabric E2: 8½" × 43½"

Background fabric: 8½" × 2½"

29

Assembling the Stripes

Press after each step.

1. Assemble Sections 1–5.

2. Carefully fold the sections in half lengthwise, so you can easily cut them into long, thin strips. Make sure to fold them so all the sides and folds are lined up and square.

3. Once the sections are folded, cut each section into 3 strips as indicated.

Section 1

2 strips 2½″ wide (1.1 and 1.2)

1 strip 3½″ wide (1.3)

Section 2

2 strips 2½″ wide (2.1 and 2.2)

1 strip 3½″ wide (2.3)

Section 3

1 strip 4½″ wide (3.3)

2 strips 3½″ wide (3.1 and 3.2)

Section 4

1 strip 3½″ wide (4.1)

2 strips 2½″ wide (4.2 and 4.3)

Section 5

1 strip 3½″ wide (5.1)

2 strips 2½″ wide (5.2 and 5.3)

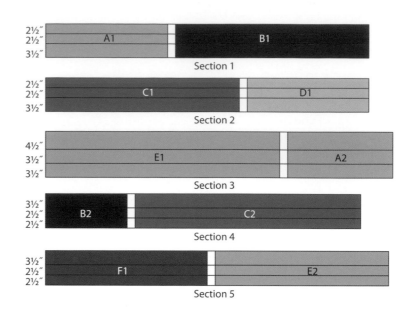

4. Now that all the stripes are the correct widths, they need to be trimmed to the correct lengths. Because you want the "break" in the stripes to be offset, you must trim them to specific lengths. Trim a specific amount off one end and then trim off enough so the finished stripes measure 70″ long.

1.1: Only cutting Fabric A, trim to 70″.

1.2: Trim Fabric A to 25½″; then trim the stripe (cutting Fabric B) to 70″.

1.3: Only cutting Fabric B, trim to 70″.

2.1: Only cutting Fabric C, trim to 70″.

2.2: Trim Fabric C to 43½″; then trim the stripe (cutting off of Fabric D) to 70″.

2.3: Only cutting Fabric D, trim to 70″.

3.1: Only cutting Fabric A, trim to 70″.

3.2: Trim Fabric E to 50½″; then trim the stripe (cutting Fabric A) to 70″.

3.3: Only cutting Fabric E, trim to 70″.

4.1: Only cutting Fabric C, trim to 70″.

4.2: Only cutting Fabric B, trim to 70".

4.3: Trim Fabric B to 15½"; then trim the stripe (cutting Fabric C) to 70".

5.1: Only cutting Fabric F, trim to 70".

5.2: Trim Fabric F to 35½", then trim the stripe (cutting Fabric E) to 70".

5.3: Only cutting Fabric E, trim to 70".

5. Carefully following the diagram, piece together the stripes of each section with the appropriate widths of background fabric strips (indicated in diagram below).

6. Once the sections are assembled, sew them to each other as indicated in the diagram.

7. Sew the top and bottom panels to the quilt top.

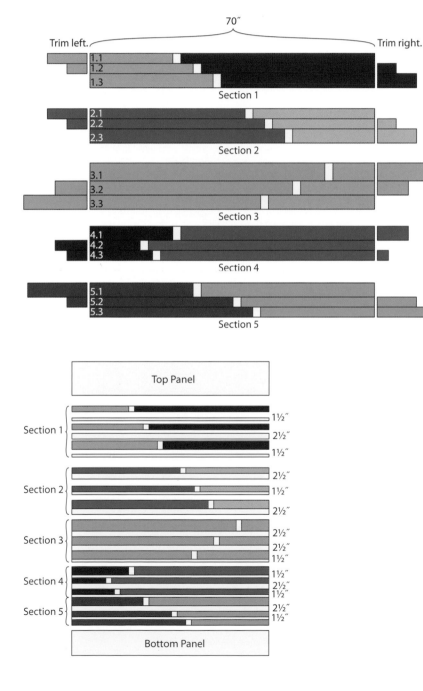

Making the Quilt Back

To make an 80″ × 90″ quilt back, cut 2 pieces 80″ × WOF and remove the selvages. Sew the 2 pieces together along the 80″ edges. Then add 10″ more to the bottom as follows: Cut 2 strips 10½″ × WOF, piece them together, trim to 80″, and then sew the long strip to the bottom of the quilt back.

Quilting Options

OPTION 1

OPTION 2

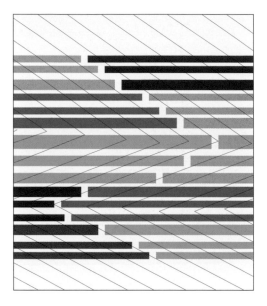

I quilted this throw in a very simple and easy wavy pattern that lends itself to this horizontal design. Each stripe got one double wavy line. I turned the quilt on its side, started in the middle of the quilt, and worked my way out to the right (the bottom of the quilt). First, I sewed one wave, then I echoed it with a second line of stitching, using the edge of my walking foot as a guide to keep them evenly spaced. I repeated this on each stripe, as well as every strip of background fabric, working my way to the bottom. Then, I rotated the whole quilt 180° and worked my way out to the top.

A very different choice for the quilting on this pattern is to sew straight lines that mirror the "breaks" in the stripes on the quilt. If it helps, use a washable marking pen or chalk to draw the first zigzag line. Angle the lines so they run through the breaks in each stripe as much as possible. Then, use a walking foot to quilt along the marking. Echo quilt the first zigzag on both sides of the quilt: Work your way from that center line out to the right, and then rotate the quilt 180° and repeat for the other side.

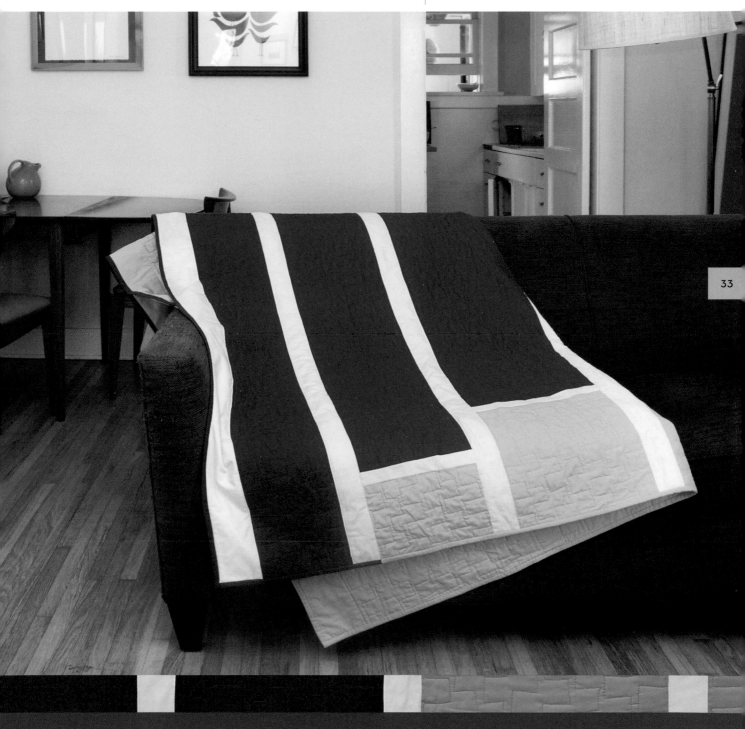

This large lap quilt is perfect for cuddling under while on the couch. The bright colors have a strong impact and complement a room with simple, contemporary design.

The big panels of fabric that make up this quilt cause it to sew up quickly and easily. Make sure you cut carefully so that the design lines up correctly.

WHAT YOU NEED

Based on 42" fabric width.

Fabric A (red): 2¾ yards

Fabric B (aqua): 1⅜ yards

Fabric C (ivory): 1⅜ yards for background

Backing: 4¾ yards

Binding: ⅞ yard

Please be sure to read Notes on Making the Quilts in This Book (page 6). Label the pieces as you cut.

CUTTING

Fabric A (red)

1. Cut 2 strips 7½" × WOF and sew them together end to end; trim A1.

2. Cut 2 strips 9½" × WOF and sew them together end to end; trim A2.

3. Cut 2 strips 13½" × WOF and sew them together end to end; trim A4.

4. Cut 1 strip 15½" × WOF; trim A5.

5. Trim the leftover strip from Step 3 to 11½" wide.

6. Cut 1 strip 11½" × WOF; sew it end to end with the strip from Step 5; trim A3.

A1: 7½" × 75½"	**A4:** 13½" × 49½"
A2: 9½" × 68½"	**A5:** 15½" × 39½"
A3: 11½" × 62½"	

Fabric B (aqua)

1. Cut 15½" from the yardage parallel to the selvage; trim B4.

2. Cut 13½" from the yardage parallel to the selvage; trim B3.

3. Cut B2.

4. Cut B1.

B1: 9½" × 6½"

B2: 11½" × 12½"

B3: 13½" × 25½"

B4: 15½" × 35½"

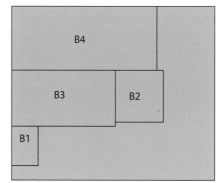

Fabric C (ivory)

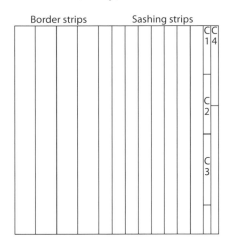

1. Cut 4 strips 4″ × WOF and sew end to end; trim to 4″ × 75½″ for the 2 border strips.

2. Cut 8 strips 2½″ × WOF and sew in pairs end to end to make 4 sashing strips. Trim to 75½″ after piecing (see Tip, below).

3. Cut 2 strips 1½″ × WOF; trim to:

C1: 1½″ × 9½″   C3: 1½″ × 13½″

C2: 1½″ × 11½″   C4: 1½″ × 15½″

Assembling the Quilt Top

Press after each step.

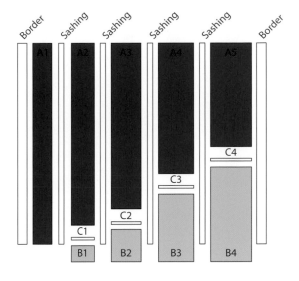

1. Sew A2, C1, and B1 into a long strip.

2. Repeat Step 1 to assemble A3, C2, B2; A4, C3, B3; and A5, C4, B4.

3. Working from left to right, assemble the quilt top.

4. Trim as necessary to square up the quilt top.

TIP

In general, when piecing long strips, it's often easier for a too-long piece of fabric to be trimmed down once it has been sewn on. When cutting, think ahead and try to leave strips longer than they need to be if the pattern allows for it. Only trim them down to their perfect length after they are sewn to the pieces of fabric that surround them. This way, you are guaranteed long enough strips, rather than ones that are ¼″ too short because of small discrepancies in your piecing or cutting. We are humans and not machines—these discrepancies happen but won't cause problems if you just think ahead in this fashion. There is nothing worse than having to tear out a very long seam because you cut your piece of fabric a bit too short, when you could have just kept it extra long.

The more you piece quilt tops, ideas such as this one will become second nature to you. These ideas are also what make quilting a more relaxing and fun process that doesn't have to be about being a fussy perfectionist.

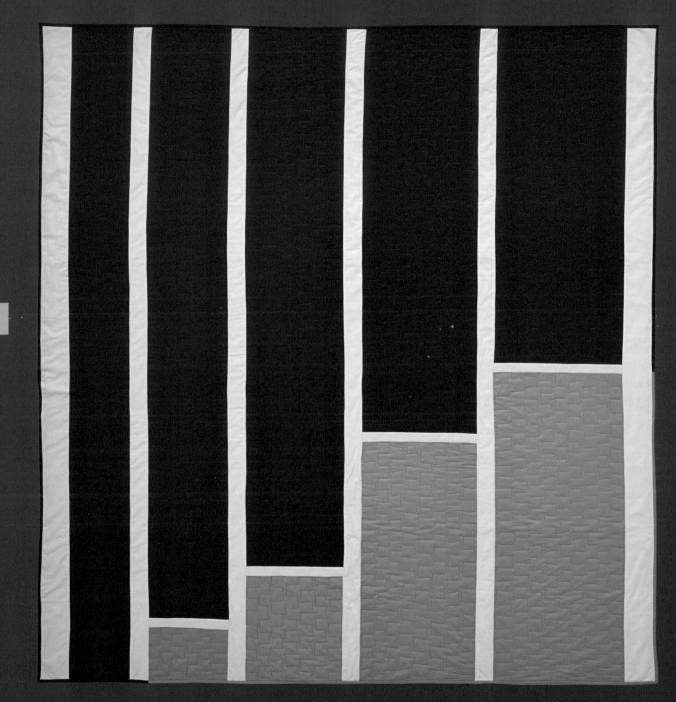

Making the Quilt Back

To make an 80″ × 84″ quilt back, cut 2 pieces 80″ × WOF and remove the selvages. Sew the 2 pieces together along the 80″ edges.

Quilting Options

OPTION 1

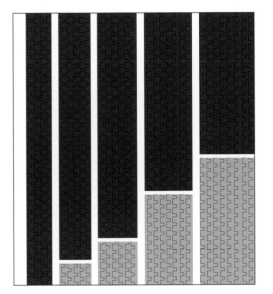

To keep the "mod" look of this quilt going, I quilted it in a boxy free-motion pattern that, when repeated, creates a square vine look.

I started in the center of the quilt and worked my way to the right, stitching in rows from top to bottom, and intentionally offsetting the lines so that each "box" didn't line up with the previous line. I worked my way from top to bottom. Then, I rotated the quilt 180° and worked my way from the center to the right.

With each row, when I came to the end of the red, I sewed a locking stitch (backstitch), lifted the presser foot, moved down to the blue fabric, sewed another locking stitch, and continued sewing the boxy vine down the blue. See a close-up of the actual quilting (page 38).

OPTION 2

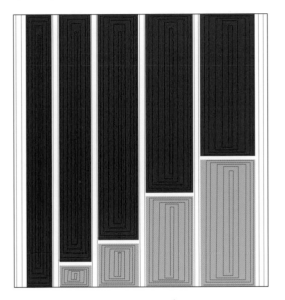

Another way to quilt this design is to fill in each blue and red column with large, straight-line spirals. Then add some vertical lines in the sashing and border. Start with the center-most column and fill in the spirals using a walking foot and turning the quilt through the machine. If your machine is small, this can be a physical task, but it can be done! Once you've filled one column of blue and red, add the vertical lines on either side of that column in the sashing. Work your way out from the center on one side, and then rotate the whole quilt 180° and fill in the other side, again working out from the center.

37

Finishing

Bind your quilt according to the instructions in Binding (page 140).

If you'd like to bind this quilt as I did—with 2 colors switching and matching up with the piecing—make 93½" of blue binding and 211½" of red binding. Piece the 2 colors together with a straight seam. Usually I sew binding strips together with diagonal seams, but this time I wanted the look of the straight seams suddenly switching the colors.

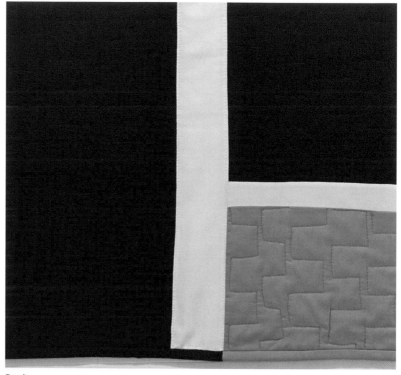

Binding

When attaching the binding, first pin it in place. Work your way around the entire edge of the quilt, lining up the color-change seam with the quilt design. Piece together the ends, again butting them up end to end and making sure you've lined up the colors correctly.

COLORFUL NEGATIVE SPACE

ART DECO | 90″ × 90″

CUTTING

This quilt has a *lot* of long strips of varying widths and lengths to deal with. Because many strips are of the same width, you will use a technique that makes measuring and cutting much easier. First, you will cut a set number of WOF (selvage to selvage) strips. Then, you will sew them all together end to end. Once they are all sewn into one incredibly long strip, you will trim it to the measured lengths of all the pieces for the quilt top. This makes piecing the strips much faster, because you don't have to think through how many WOF strips each piece needs. Instead, you just sew them all together and trim to the correct lengths. Label each piece as you cut it to prevent confusion.

Fabric A (aqua)

1. Cut 2 strips 24½" × WOF (selvage to selvage) and sew together end to end; cut A1 and A2.

2. Cut 5 strips 2½" × WOF. Trim 1 strip to A5. Sew the remaining 4 strips together end to end; cut A7 and A9.

3. Cut 5 strips 6½" × WOF and sew together end to end; cut A4, A6, and A8.

4. Cut 3 strips 4½" × WOF and sew together end to end; cut A10.

5. Cut A3 from the remaining fabric.

A1: 24½" × 49½"	A5: 2½" × 41½"	A9: 2½" × 79½"
A2: 24½" × 30½"	A6: 6½" × 60½"	A10: 4½" × 90"
A3: 24½" × 11½"	A7: 2½" × 60½"	
A4: 6½" × 41½"	A8: 6½" × 79½"	

This is the first of the queen-size quilt patterns. The stepped pattern lends itself to any stylish bedroom. Why not make it in a daring color palette to add an amazing hand-made touch to your bedroom decor? Nothing is more satisfying than going to sleep each night under a quilt that you made.

Tackling a quilt this large can seem daunting, but this is just the sort of pattern to choose as your first large quilt. Piecing this quilt top is a touch more time consuming than some of the other patterns in this book, but it's still very straightforward and manageable for a beginner. Doing the actual quilting of a quilt this large might be the hardest part, but you should dive in and take on the challenge!

WHAT YOU NEED

Based on 42" fabric width.

Fabric A (aqua): 3½ yards

Fabric B (gray): 2¼ yards

Fabric C (teal blue): 2 yards

Backing: 7¼ yards

Binding: 1 yard

Please be sure to read Notes on Making the Quilts in This Book (page 6).

Fabric B (gray)

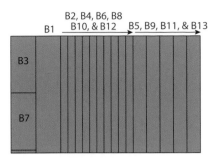

1. Cut 2 strips 8½″ × WOF; cut B1 (first), B3, and B7.

2. Cut 10 strips 2½″ × WOF and sew together end to end into a very, very, *very* long strip; cut B2, B4, B6, B8, B10, and B12.

3. Cut 6 strips 4½″ × WOF and sew together end to end; cut B5, B9, B11, and B13.

B1: 8½″ × 41½″	B8: 2½″ × 60½″
B2: 2½″ × 41½″	B9: 4½″ × 60½″
B3: 8½″ × 19½″	B10: 2½″ × 79½″
B4: 2½″ × 41½″	B11: 4½″ × 11½″
B5: 4½″ × 41½″	B12: 2½″ × 79½″
B6: 2½″ × 60½″	B13: 4½″ × 90″
B7: 8½″ × 19½″	

Fabric C (teal blue)

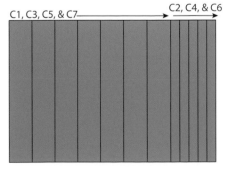

1. Cut 7 strips 6½″ × WOF and sew together end to end into a very long strip; cut C1, C3, C5, and C7.

2. Cut 5 strips 2½″ × WOF and sew together end to end; cut C2, C4, and C6.

C1: 6½″ × 41½″	C5: 6½″ × 79½″
C2: 2½″ × 41½″	C6: 2½″ × 79½″
C3: 6½″ × 60½″	C7: 6½″ × 90″
C4: 2½″ × 60½″	

Sewing the Sections

Press after each step.

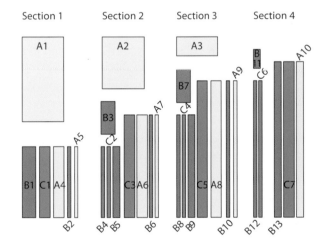

Assembling the Quilt Top

Sew together Sections 1, 2, 3, and 4 as shown above to complete the top.

43

Making the Quilt Back

To make a 100″ × 100″ quilt back, cut 2 pieces 100″ × WOF and remove the selvages. Sew the 2 pieces together along the 100″ edges. Then add 16″ more to the bottom as follows: Cut 3 strips 16½″ × WOF, piece them together, trim to 100″, and sew the long strip to the bottom of the quilt back.

Quilting Options

OPTION 1

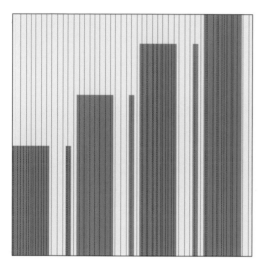

OPTION 2

I really wanted to stick with the design's straight-line graphic nature and draw attention to the negative space to make the pattern stand out.

I quilted straight vertical lines on the entire face of the quilt, filling in the gray and teal with dense quilting lines (½″ apart) and the background aqua half as densely (1″ apart).

I started in the center of the quilt and worked to the right. When a gray or teal piece started below the aqua, I put my needle in where I wanted to start the line, sewed a couple of locking stitches, and continued down the quilt. Once I completed one side of the quilt, I rotated it 180° and worked on the other side, again gradually working my way to the right. See a close-up of the actual quilting (page 134).

Another allover straight-line quilting option is to echo the piecing with "steps." Once you've sewn the first set of steps by following the piecing, you can simply echo them for the subsequent set and so on. Use a quilting bar to keep the lines equidistant. Work your way out on one side of the quilt; then rotate it 180° and work your way out on the other half.

This incredibly simple quilt is the ideal gift for that friend who is a lover of neutrals. This throw will add just the smallest pop of color, but a lot of sophistication, to any couch. For the background fabric, I used some lovely natural linen that has a wonderful texture and adds a great weight and drape to the quilt.

Quilting with linen can prove to be a touch difficult. It doesn't "stick" to cotton batting the way quilting cottons do, and it can shift more as you quilt through the layers. I pin baste more densely than normal to compensate for this shifting. This could be an opportunity to try spray basting to see if you like it (page 133).

WHAT YOU NEED

Based on 42" fabric width.

Fabric A (light brown): 2¾ yards (60"-wide linen)
or 3⅜ yards (42"-wide cotton) for background*

Fabric B (tan): ⅝ yard

Fabric C (red): 14½" × 13½"

Backing: 4¼ yards

Binding: ⅞ yard

**Because linen comes wider than quilting cottons, fabric requirements and cutting instructions for both are included here.*

Please be sure to read Notes on Making the Quilts in This Book (page 6). Label the pieces as you cut.

CUTTING

Fabric A (light brown)

LINEN

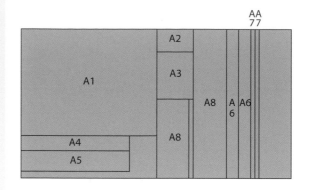

1. Cut 49½" × WOF; cut A1 (first), A4, and A5.

2. Cut 1 strip 13½" × WOF; cut A2 and A3. Trim the leftover fabric to 12½" wide.

3. Cut 1 strip 12½" × WOF and sew to the leftover strip from Step 2 end to end; cut A8.

4. Cut 2 strips 4½" × WOF and sew together end to end; cut A6.

5. Cut 2 strips 1½" × WOF and sew together end to end; cut A7.

A1: 39½" × 49½"   A5: 39½" × 7½"

A2: 8½" × 13½"   A6: 4½" × 75"

A3: 17½" × 13½"   A7: 1½" × 75"

A4: 39½" × 5½"   A8: 12½" × 75"

COTTON

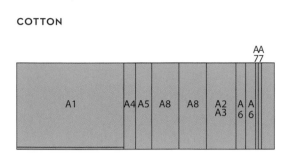

1. Cut 49½" × WOF; cut A1.

2. Cut 1 strip 5½" × WOF; cut A4.

3. Cut 1 strip 7½" × WOF; cut A5.

4. Cut 2 strips 12½" × WOF and sew together end to end; cut A8.

5. Cut 1 strip 13½" × WOF; cut A2 and A3.

6. Cut 2 strips 4½" × WOF and sew together end to end; cut A6.

7. Cut 2 strips 1½" × WOF and sew together end to end; cut A7.

Fabric B (tan)

1. Cut 2 strips 2½" × WOF and sew together end to end; cut B1.

2. Cut 6 strips 1½" × WOF and sew together end to end in pairs; cut B2, B3, and B4.

B1: 2½" × 75"	B3: 1½" × 75"
B2: 1½" × 75"	B4: 1½" × 60½"

Fabric C (red)

This piece is already cut.

Sewing the Panels

Press after each step.

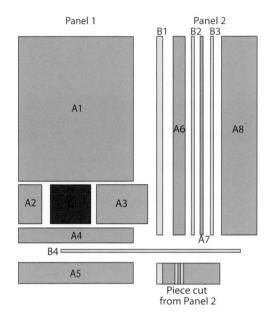

Piece cut from Panel 2

PANEL 1

1. Sew together A2, C, and A3.

2. Add A1.

3. Add A4.

PANEL 2

1. Sew together B1, A6, B2, A7, B3, and A8.

2. Press well and cut 7½" from the bottom; set the 7½" piece aside.

Assembling the Quilt Top

1. Sew Panel 1 to Panel 2.

2. Sew the 7½" piece from Panel 2 that you cut off to A5 end to end.

3. Add B4.

4. Sew this section to Panel 1/2.

Making the Quilt Back

To make a 70″ × 84″ quilt back, cut 2 pieces 70″ × WOF and remove the selvages. Sew the 2 pieces together along the 70″ edges.

Quilting Options

OPTION 1

OPTION 2

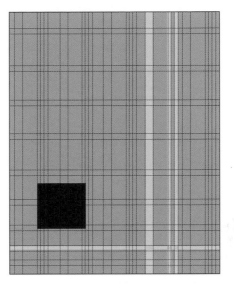

I covered the entire quilt in a dense spiral to add some interest to the minimal design. First, I measured the quilt to find the center, which is where I started the spiral. With a marking pen or chalk (something that will wash off!), I carefully drew the beginning of the spiral on the quilt. There is no need to draw all the many rounds of the spiral.

Because the spiral in the very center of the quilt requires tight turns, I sewed the center rounds with a free-motion foot, carefully following the spiral lines I had drawn. When I came to the end of my drawn line, I switched to a walking foot and sewed the remainder of the spiral, using the edge of the foot as a guide to keep the widths of each round uniform. When the spiral was so big that I was sewing off the edges of the quilt (which happens, because the quilt is a rectangle), I echoed the spiral quilting lines to fill in the corners of the quilt.

Another quilting option is to echo the lines created in the piecing and repeat them over the quilt. Since these are all straight lines and because linen can be shiftier than cotton, make sure you've basted densely (or spray basted) before you quilt. First, fill in all the horizontal seams. Then, fill in all the vertical ones. Should you find the fabric shifting, slow down and adjust the presser foot to a lighter pressure setting if your machine allows for it.

TIP

It might be smart to test on a scrap sandwich how many rounds of the spiral you need to sew before your walking foot can take the turns smoothly.

PICK UP STICKS | 80" × 85"

Note *Pieces that are labeled with a ".1" indicate that they are initially cut with their counterparts and are then trimmed off later.*

CUTTING

Fabric A (blue)

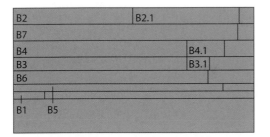

1. Cut 1 strip 10½" parallel to the selvage; cut A1, A2, A3, A4, and A5.

TIP Make sure you fold your fabric carefully before you cut. Line up the selvage so you know it's square and your strips will be nice and straight.

2. Cut 1 strip 25½" parallel to the selvage; cut A8, A9, A10, and A11.

3. From the remaining fabric from Step 2, cut A6, A7, and A12.

A1: 12½" × 10½"	A5: 58½" × 10½"	A9: 58½" × 25½"
A2: 26½" × 10½"	A6: 4½" × 5½"	A10: 12½" × 25½"
A3: 35½" × 10½"	A7: 5½" × 4½"	A11: 58½" × 25½"
A4: 12½" × 10½"	A8: 12½" × 25½"	A12: 5½" × 10½"

Fabric B (yellow)

1. Cut 3 strips 5½" wide parallel to the selvage.

2. From a 5½" strip, cut B2 and B2.1.

Just two fabrics are used to make this graphic, eye-catching, double-size quilt.

The piecing of this quilt, like many others in this book, is not as involved as it looks. Many of the sections are the same, enabling you to piece long strips and then cut them into different portions and reassemble them with the remainder of the quilt top.

WHAT YOU NEED

Based on 42" fabric width.

Fabric A (blue): 4½ yards

Fabric B (yellow): 2¼ yards

Backing: 6¼ yards

Binding: ⅞ yard

Please be sure to read Notes on Making the Quilts in This Book (page 6). Label the pieces as you cut.

3. From another 5½" strip, cut B7.

4. From the last of the 5½" strips, cut B4 and B4.1.

5. Cut 2 strips 4½" wide parallel to the selvage.

6. From a 4½" strip, cut B3 and B3.1.

7. Working with the last 4½"-wide strip, cut B6.

8. Cut 1 strip 2½" wide parallel to the selvage; cut B5.

9. Cut B1.

B1: 2½" × 10½"

B2: 5½" × 40½"

B2.1: 5½" × 35½"

B3: 4½" × 58½"

B3.1: 4½" × 7½"

B4: 5½" × 58½"

B4.1: 5½" × 12½"

B5: 2½" × 70½"

B6: 4½" × 65½"

B7: 5½" × 75½"

Assembling the Quilt Top

Press after each step.

We'll assemble some strips, cut them up, and then assemble the remainder of the quilt top.

1. Sew A5, B3, A9, B4, and A11.

2. Cut this strip set into 3 panels: 12½" wide (Panel 1), 10½" wide (Panel 2), and 35½" wide (Panel 3).

3. Sew A1, B1, and A2.

4. Sew B2 to the bottom of this unit (Panel 4).

5. Sew A7 to B3.1.

6. Sew A4, A7/B3.1, A8, B4.1, and A10 (Panel 5).

7. Sew A6 to B6 (Panel 6).

8. Sew B7 to A12 (Panel 7).

9. Assemble Panel 5, B5, Panel 1, Panel 6, and Panel 2.

10. Sew Panel 4 to the top of the unit from Step 9.

11. Sew Panel 7 to the right side and set aside.

12. Sew A3, B2.1, and Panel 3.

13. Sew the 2 sides of the quilt together and your quilt top is all done!

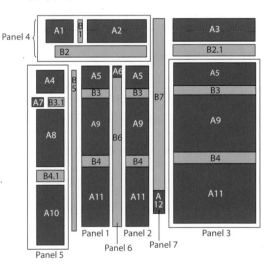

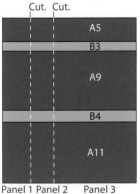

Cut. Cut.

Panel 1   Panel 2   Panel 3
12½"   10½"   35½"

Making the Quilt Back

To make a 90" × 95" quilt back, cut 2 pieces 90" × WOF and remove the selvages. Sew the 2 pieces together along the 90" edges. Then add 11" more to the bottom as follows: Cut 3 strips 11½" × WOF, piece them together, trim to 90", and sew the long strip to the bottom of the quilt back.

Quilting Options

OPTION 1

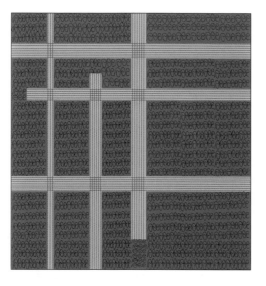

OPTION 2

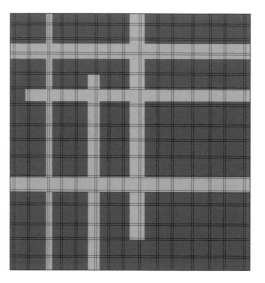

For this quilt, I mixed straight-line and free-motion quilting. In order not to draw attention away from the design, I quilted the yellow with a pale yellow thread and the blue with a blue thread.

First, I filled in all the dense, straight-line quilting with a walking foot. I used the edge of the foot as a guide to keep the lines evenly spaced. Then, I switched to a free-motion foot. In rows along the quilt, I filled in the blue areas of the quilt in a wave-like repeat pattern.

When I came to a yellow area of the quilt, I finished a wave, sewed a locking stitch, picked up the presser foot, and moved the quilt to the left on the other side of the yellow. Then, I sewed a locking stitch again and continued. When I was done, I clipped all the running threads.

Another quilting option that does not detract from the piecing design is simply to cover the quilt in a very straightforward plaid pattern. Sets of 2 straight lines, with each set spaced 5"–6" apart, make up the pattern. First, fill in all the straight vertical lines, working from the top to the bottom of the quilt. Work from the center of the quilt out to the right. Then, rotate the quilt 180° and fill in the other side. Once all the vertical lines are in, repeat the process with horizontal lines.

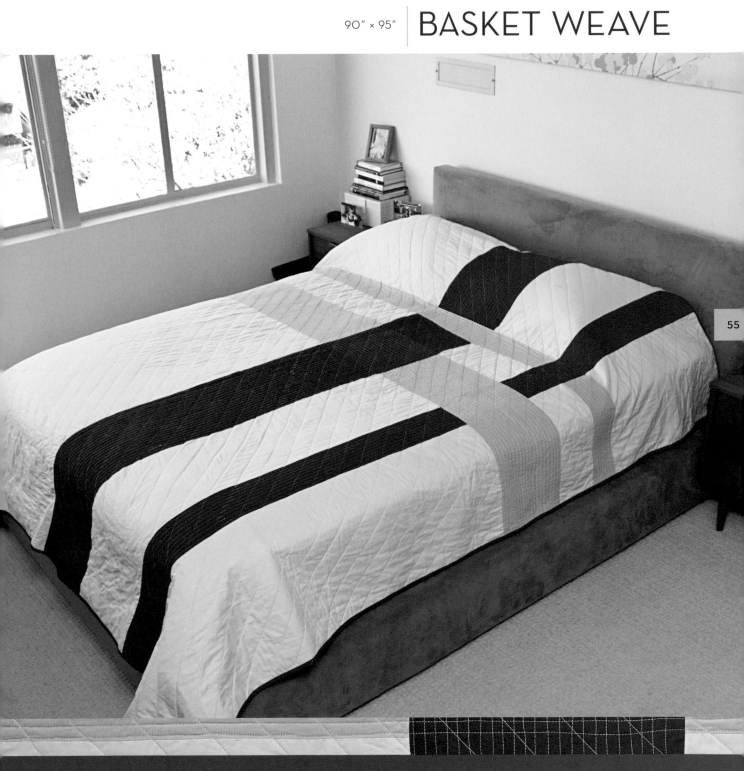

BASKET WEAVE

This fun plaid quilt is big enough for a queen-size bed. Making a large bed quilt is definitely more time consuming than making a smaller quilt, but when it is this quick to piece, it's a very manageable task to take on. Why not make this quilt in darker colors for a simple masculine design that your favorite guy is certain to love?

WHAT YOU NEED

Based on 42" fabric width.

Fabric A (aqua): 4⅝ yards for background

Fabric B (tan): 1⅛ yards

Fabric C (red): 1½ yards

Backing: 7⅝ yards

Binding: ⅞ yard

CUTTING

Fabric A (aqua)

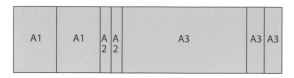

1. Cut 2 strips 25½" × WOF (selvage to selvage) and sew together end to end; trim A1.

2. Cut 2 strips 6½" × WOF and sew together end to end; trim A2.

3. Cut 1 piece 40½" × 74½".

4. Cut 2 strips 10½" × WOF and sew together end to end; trim to 74½".

5. Sew the pieces from Steps 3 and 4 together along the long side to make A3.

   A1: 25½" × 74½" (After some piecing, this will be cut down to A1, A1.1, and A1.2.)

   A2: 6½" × 74½" (After some piecing, this will be cut down to A2, A2.1, and A2.2.)

   A3: 50½" × 74½"
   Cut into A3: 50½" × 45½"; A3.1: 50½" × 12½"; and A3.2: 50½" × 16½".

Fabric B (tan)

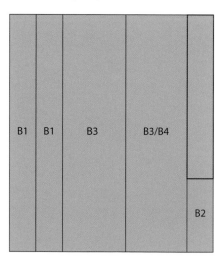

1. Cut 2 strips 4½" × WOF and sew together end to end; trim B1.

2. Cut 2 strips 10½" × WOF and sew together end to end; cut B3 and B4.

3. Cut B2.

B1: 4½" × 74½"
(After some piecing, this will be cut down to B1, B1.1, and B1.2.)

B2: 4½" × 12½"

B3: 10½" × 45½"

B4: 10½" × 33½"

Fabric C (red)

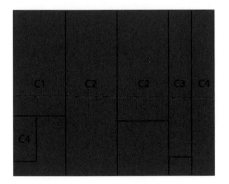

1. Cut 3 strips 12½" × WOF.

2. Trim a strip from Step 1 to C1. Set aside the leftover strip.

3. Sew together the 2 other 12½" strips end to end; cut C2.

4. Cut 2 strips 5½" × WOF.

5. Trim a strip from Step 4 to C3.

6. Trim the scrap from Step 2 to 5½" × 11" and sew this scrap to the remaining 5½"-wide strip; cut C4.

C1: 12½" × 25½"

C2: 12½" × 66½"

C3: 5½" × 35½"

C4: 5½" × 50½"

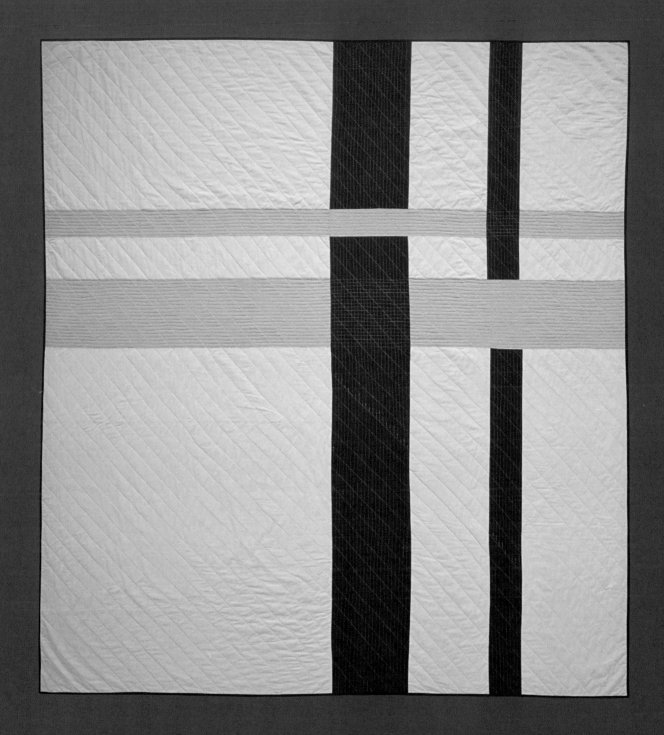

Assembling the Quilt Top

Press after each step.

Strips are sewn together, and then those units are cut into sections to make the quilt top.

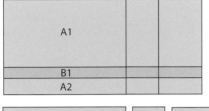

1. Sew A1, B1, and A2.

2. Cut the strip set from Step 1 into 3 units: 45½" wide, 12½" wide, and 16½" wide.

3. Add B3 and A3 to the 45½"-wide unit (Panel 1).

4. Sew C1, B2, and C2 (Panel 2).

5. Sew A1.1 / B1.1 / A2.1 to C3 and then add A1.2 / B1.2 / A2.2 (Panel 3).

6. Sew A3.1 and A3.2 to C4 (Panel 4).

7. Sew Panels 3 and 4 to B4.

8. Sew Panels 1 and 2 together.

9. Sew the 2 halves together to complete the quilt top.

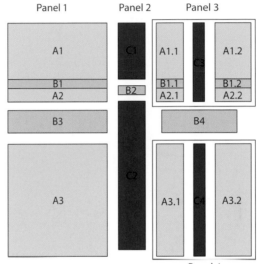

Making the Quilt Back

To make a 100" × 105" quilt back, cut 2 pieces 100" × WOF and remove the selvages. Sew the 2 pieces together along the 100" edges. Then add 21" more to the bottom as follows: Cut 3 strips 21½" × WOF, piece them together, trim to 100", and sew the long strip to the bottom of the quilt back.

Quilting Options

OPTION 1

OPTION 2

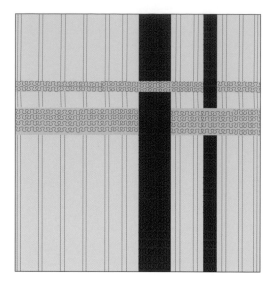

I quilted in an allover diagonal straight-line pattern. Then, I quilted vertical and horizontal lines over the pieced stripes to emphasize the design.

To make the first center diagonal line straight, I placed the basted quilt on the floor and used chalk to mark the longest central line from one corner to the other. Then, I followed that chalk line when sewing the first line of quilting through the quilt. I used a quilting bar on my sewing machine to keep the rest of the lines a uniform 2" apart. I worked my way out from the center of the quilt in one direction. When I reached the outer corner, I rotated the quilt and started working my way out from the center on the other side.

Once I finished the allover quilting, I added the vertical and then horizontal lines along the pieced strips. I used the edge of the pieced strip as a guide to make the first line straight, and then I used the edge of the walking foot to guide each line of quilting from there.

Another choice of quilting for this pattern is to mix free-motion quilting with straight-line quilting. First, fill in the plaid piecing with an allover free-motion meandering pattern. Then, switch to a walking foot and fill in all the negative space with straight-line quilting. Start in the center of the quilt and work your way out to the right. Be sure to use locking stitches every time you get to the plaid piecing and start back on the negative space. When you finish the first half of the quilt, rotate it 180° and work your way out from the center again.

IMPROVISATIONAL PIECING

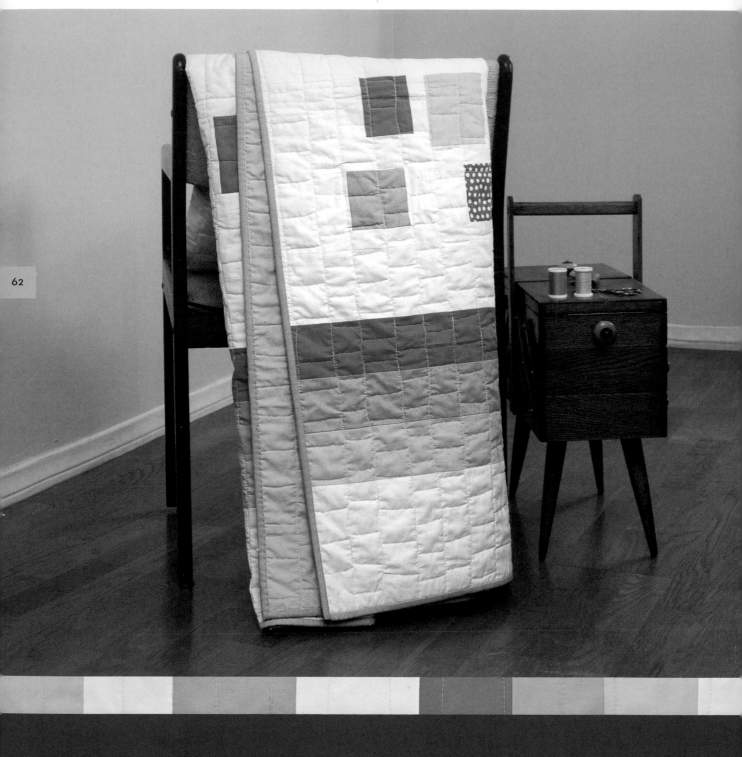

CUTTING

Fabric A (white)

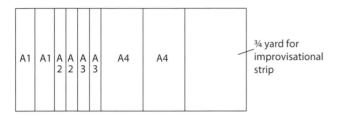

³⁄₄ yard for improvisational strip

1. Cut 2 strips 7½″ × WOF (selvage to selvage) and sew end to end; trim A1.

2. Cut 4 strips 4½″ × WOF and sew end to end; trim A2 and A3.

3. Cut 2 strips 16½″ × WOF and sew end to end; trim A4.

4. Cut 1 strip of each of the following sizes for the improv section: 1½″ × WOF, 2½″ × WOF, and 3½″ × WOF.

A1: 7½″ × 80″	A3: 4½″ × 80″	**Improv section:**
A2: 4½″ × 80″	A4: 16½″ × 80″	1½″ × WOF, 2½″ × WOF, and 3½″ × WOF

This bright and sunny quilt design is perfect for any child's room. Since it's twin size, why not make it for your son's or daughter's bed?

This is the first quilt in this book that involves some improvisational piecing (see page 130). The improv section of the quilt will take the most time to piece. Take your time—embrace and enjoy the process and make the quilt top your own by knowing that no one is making a quilt identical to yours.

WHAT YOU NEED

Based on 42″ fabric width.

Fabric A (white): 3 yards for background

Fabric B, C, and D (yellow, green, orange): ³⁄₄ yard of each

Backing: 4⅞ yards

Binding: ⅞ yard

Please be sure to read Notes on Making the Quilts in This Book (page 6). Label the pieces as you cut.

MODERN MINIMAL

Cutting, continued

Fabrics B, C, and D (yellow, green, and orange)

1. Cut 4 strips 3½" × WOF and sew in pairs end to end to make 2 long strips; trim B1 from one strip and B2 from the other strip.

2. Repeat Step 1 with Fabrics C and D.

3. Stack the remaining yardage of all 3 fabrics and cut out about 10 squares and rectangles of various sizes, ranging from 3" to 6". The shapes do not have to be perfectly square; having ever-so-slight angles in your cuts can create some interesting imperfection. This is often called "wonky" piecing.

> B1 and B2: 3½" × 80"
>
> C1 and C2: 3½" × 80"
>
> D1 and D2: 3½" × 80"

TIP

There are different methods for making varying degrees of wonky piecing. Try different things to see what works for you: Cut with your rotary cutter but no ruler; cut with scissors. Try different ways to push yourself out of your perfectly square comfort zone!

Assembling the Quilt Top

Press after each step.

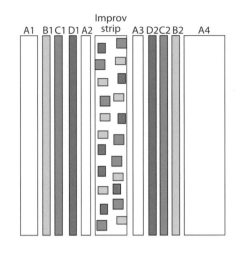

IMPROV SECTION

When making this section of the quilt, you should feel completely free to make it your own. Have fun with piecing and finding your own style.

1. Using the background fabric strips, cut off pieces to sew onto the green, yellow, and orange squares and rectangles.

TIP

For me, the section came together easily when I thought of it as being 5 blocks 16½" × 16½" that I assembled in a long strip.

2. To make each "block," lay out 4 or 5 rectangles and then cut a sufficient number of the right size and width of background pieces to surround all the rectangles in white. I don't measure to do this; I just eyeball it. Always err on the side of cutting the background fabric too big. With each seam you sew, trim down the edge so it's straight (not necessarily square, but straight). This makes it easier to sew the next piece of fabric. With enough precut background pieces, you can sew together a part of the improv section without having to stop to cut the correct length of background fabric for each seam.

TIP

When I improv piece in this fashion, I often don't sit down at my sewing machine. Instead, I stand and move from my cutting mat to my sewing machine, to my ironing board, and back to my cutting mat. This cut, sew, press, trim, cut, sew, press, trim process has become second nature to me and will to you too with some practice. Plus, I like to fool myself into thinking that this makes quilting a calorie-burning endeavor!

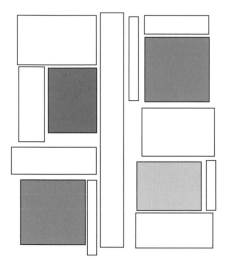

3. As you finish each unit of 4 or 5 squares, trim it to 16½" wide.

4. Continue piecing the rectangles and the background fabric as needed until your finished strip measures 16½" × 80".

5. Working left to right, piece the entire quilt top by sewing A1, B1, C1, D1, A2, improv strip, A3, D2, C2, B2, and A4 together, in that order.

Making the Quilt Back

To make a 75" × 90" quilt back, cut 2 pieces 75" × WOF and remove the selvages. Sew the 2 pieces together along the 75" edges. Add 6" more to the bottom as following: Cut 2 strips 6½" × WOF, piece them together, trim to 75", and sew the long strip to the bottom of the quilt back.

Quilting Options

OPTION 1

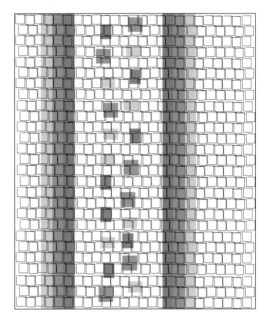

OPTION 2

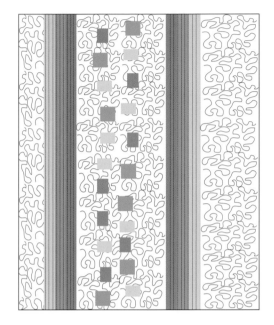

I quilted an allover free-motion pattern made up of rows of squares. This quilting not only added to the quilt's cobblestone theme but also provided wonderful texture.

With a free-motion foot, I started at the top of the quilt and filled in the entire quilt with rows of approximately 2″ × 2″ boxes. As I quilted, I back-tracked and sewed over existing quilting so that a whole row could be quilted without stopping. I offset each row of boxes, so the edge of one box is centered over the middle of a box in the row above it.

After every 2 or 3 rows of quilting, I measured to make sure that the boxes were staying relatively the same size and therefore the rows were staying straight. If I found that I was getting off by ½″ or so, I compensated for it, adjusting the box size slightly as I sewed the next row of boxes. See a close-up of the actual quilting (page 130).

If you'd like to draw more focus to the specific piecing in the quilt, you can easily stitch in-the-ditch (the seam)—(I actually prefer stitching just outside the ditch.)—around the individual "stones" that you pieced into the improv section. From there, quilt long, dense vertical lines to fill in the yellow, green, and orange piecing. Fill in the negative space with an allover stipple to add cozy texture without taking attention away from the colorful piecing.

MOSAIC | 54" × 60"

CUTTING

Background fabric (gray)

Cut 2 pieces 18½" × 54½" parallel to the selvage.

Improv fabrics (4 colors)

Cut 1 strip of each fabric of the following sizes: 4" × WOF (selvage to selvage), 5" × WOF, and 6" × WOF. (There are no set measurements for the fabric used in the improvisational piecing.)

Assembling the Quilt Top

Press after each step.

1. Arrange the improv strips in 4 different groupings of 3 strips each, mixing up the colors and widths.

2. Sew together the strips, so you have 4 strip sets.

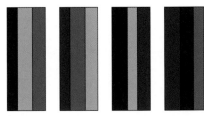

Sew strips.

WHAT YOU NEED

Based on 42" fabric width.

Gray: 1¾ yards for background

Pink to deep purple: ⅝ yard each of 4 different colors

Backing: 3⅞ yards

Binding: ¾ yard

Please be sure to read Notes on Making the Quilts in This Book (page 6). Label the pieces as you cut.

3. Stack these panels and cut each unit into 3 units 6″ wide, 2 units 5″ wide, and 3 units 4″ wide. If you like a free look, cut with your rotary cutter but don't use a ruler for this step.

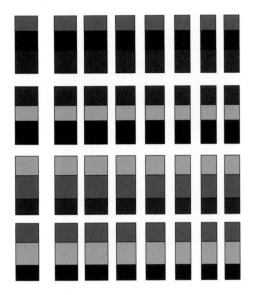

4. Assemble all the little units from Step 3 into the large center panel.

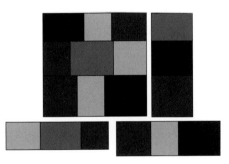

You can sew together 3 strips and then tack 1 on the side, or you can sew them into long strips and add that on. No matter how you assemble and grow the center panel, it will look great. The point here is haphazardness and winging it.

5. Once the panel measures a bit bigger than 24½″ × 54½″, square it up so it is a perfect 24½″ × 54½″ rectangle.

6. Sew the 2 background panels to the center panel and your quilt top is complete!

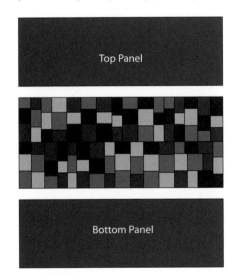

Making the Quilt Back

To make a 64″ × 70″ quilt back, cut 2 pieces 64″ × WOF and remove the selvages. Sew the 2 pieces together along the 64″ edges. Trim to 70″ long.

Quilting Options

OPTION 1

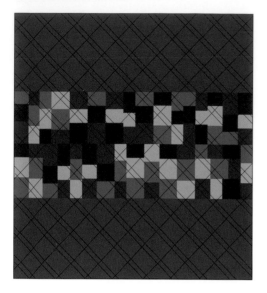

OPTION 2

I covered this quilt in an intentionally imperfect plaid straight-line quilting design. After I made this quilt top, I stumbled across some variegated thread that was the exact colors in the piecing, so I used it for the quilting.

First, I sewed a center diagonal line from corner to corner of the quilt. I was not concerned with making this quilting perfect (I love the look of the organic lines), so I just did this by sight without marking the quilt top.

Then, I worked my way to the corner of the quilt, covering it in lines spaced about 2"–3" apart. I rotated the quilt 180° and followed the same process to fill in the other half of the quilt. I then sewed an echoed line of each seam. To finish, I turned the quilt and sewed the opposite diagonal lines, but I didn't add the echoed lines. See a close-up of the actual quilting (page 135).

Because the piecing in this quilt is random, I think that an allover quilting design works best. For a soft look, free-motion quilt the entire quilt with a nice big, relaxed curlicue meandering pattern.

74

This queen-size quilt is the main feature to a bedroom. It might be big, but it goes together quickly with just one large portion of improv piecing playing the starring role.

The cluster portion of this quilt top is made with improvisational piecing. How much you make it your own or stick to the details of the pattern is completely up to you.

WHAT YOU NEED

Based on 42" fabric width.

Fabric A (green): 5½ yards

Fabric B (ivory): ¾ yard

Backing: 7¼ yards

Binding: 1 yard

Please be sure to read Notes on Making the Quilts in This Book (page 6). Label the pieces as you cut.

CUTTING

Fabric A (green)

As you cut this fabric, save all of the scraps to use as the cluster-piecing background fabric.

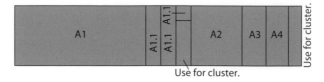

1. Cut 1 piece 90½" × WOF (selvage to selvage); trim A1.

2. Cut 3 strips 10½" × WOF and sew end to end; trim A1.1.

3. Cut 1 strip 35½" × WOF; trim A2.

4. Cut 1 strip 16½" × WOF; trim A3.

5. Cut 1 strip 15½" × WOF; trim A4.

A1: 40½" × 90½"   A3: 16½" × 40½

A1.1: 10½" × 90½"   A4: 15½" × 40½"

A2: 35½" × 40½"

6. Cut some strips for the cluster. Random-length pieces will get you started, and you can cut more as you go.

Fabric B (ivory)

Cut the cluster fabric into approximately 15 squares and rectangles that measure anywhere from 3" to 8", varying their sizes and shapes. Perfectly straight lines are not key here. Angles and wonky piecing add interest to the overall look of the cluster.

Assembling the Quilt Top

Press after each step.

MAKING THE CLUSTER

The idea behind this section of the quilt top is that you can make it your own by putting together the white pieces and the surrounding background in your own style.

If this style of "winging it" doesn't appeal to you, you can follow the exact process that I have documented here. However, I strongly encourage you to give it a shot. Don't worry about mistakes; there is no such thing in this type of piecing.

To get a free, organic look, don't be concerned with squaring up as you go. Trim the edges into straight lines so you can easily sew on the next piece, but don't square up until your piecing is in larger sections—unless, of course, you love a perfectly square look. In that case, square up as frequently as you'd like!

1. Put the randomly cut Fabric A strips next to a Fabric B piece on the cutting mat. Trim Fabric A to length, always erring on the side of cutting too long. Sew the side strips and trim. Add the bottom strip and trim.

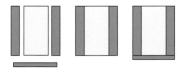

TIP

Working on a design wall helps enormously with this process. Tape or mark out a rectangle that measures 24½" × 40½" and slowly fill it in with white pieces and surrounding fabric. This is a great way to end up with a correctly sized finished cluster while also being able to design as you go without having to measure before cutting.

2. Surround a second Fabric B piece with some Fabric A and sew to the first rectangle.

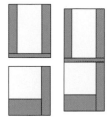

Consider pairing a couple of white blocks as you surround them.

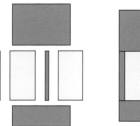

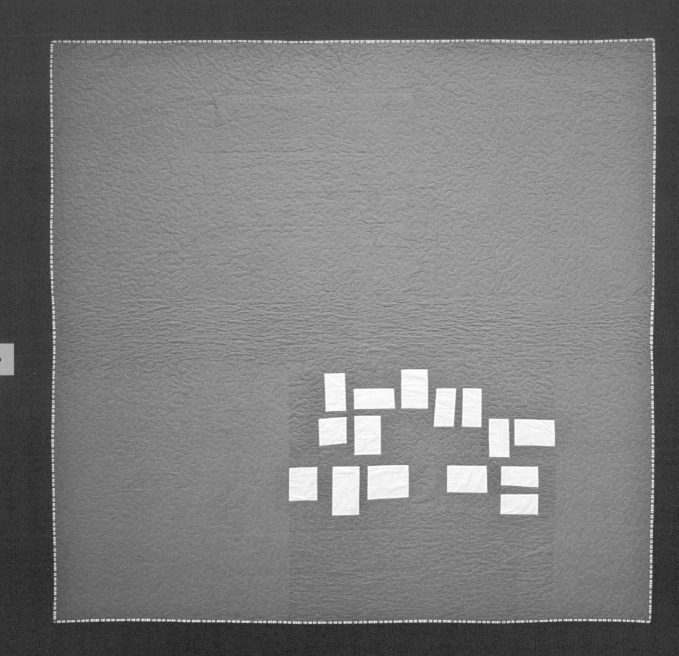

3. Continue until all the white pieces, surrounded in background fabric, are assembled and measure slightly larger than 24½″ × 40½″. Trim to 24½″ × 40½″.

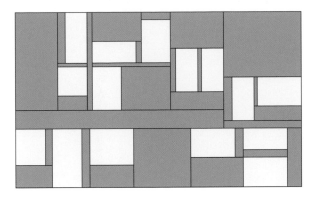

Use the cluster diagram as a guide if it helps you. However, I encourage you to get creative with this piecing. Have fun and just roll with it. If a couple of rectangles don't seem to be working out for you, chuck them, grab a couple more, and keep on going. There are no mistakes!

ADDING THE BACKGROUND FABRIC TO THE CLUSTER

1. Sew A3 to the bottom of the finished cluster.

2. Sew A2 and A4 to the sides of the A3/cluster unit.

3. Sew A1 to A1.1. Sew the 2 halves of the quilt together.

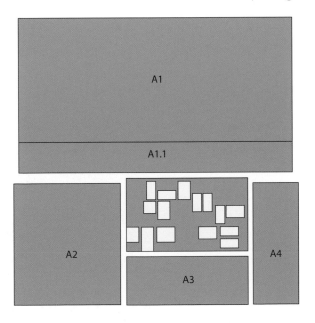

Making the Quilt Back

To make a 100″ × 100″ quilt back, cut 2 pieces 100″ × WOF and remove the selvages. Sew the 2 pieces together along the 100″ edges. Then add 16″ more to the bottom as follows: Cut 3 strips 16½″ × WOF, piece them together, trim to 100″, and sew the long strip to the bottom of the quilt back.

Quilting Options

OPTION 1

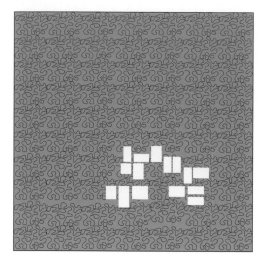

OPTION 2

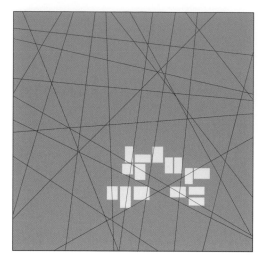

Since there is so much open space in this quilt, I filled it with an allover stippling pattern. This is a very common quilting pattern and is a great one to start with as a beginning free-motion quilter. This forgiving pattern gives a quilt a wonderful crinkle after it's been washed.

I echo quilted straight lines (stitched just outside the ditch) around the white pieces. Then, I worked my way across the quilt in an allover meandering pattern. See a close-up of the actual quilting (page 137).

A very different choice is to sew allover "crazy" straight lines. This style of quilting leads to great results and is impossible to mess up. It might be just the simple and modern way for you to get this big quilt covered in pretty quilting stitches! Go crazy and quilt as much or as little as you like. Start by putting some stabilizing lines of stitching that run all the way across the quilt in a variety of directions. Get the quilt more or less stable and then add random, denser lines everywhere you like.

This quilt is the perfect size for a throw. Maybe you'd like to make one to keep in your car so you can make use of it on a sunny day for a picnic or on trips to the beach.

This simple pattern uses an improv piecing technique and is otherwise a breeze to piece together.

WHAT YOU NEED

Based on 42" fabric width.

Fabric A (ivory): 1 yard

Fabric B (black): 1 yard

Fabric C (gold): 2⅛ yards

Fabric D (red): ⅝ yard

Fabric E (yellow): 7" × 7" scrap

Backing: 4¼ yards

Binding: ¾ yard

Please be sure to read Notes on Making the Quilts in This Book (page 6). Label the pieces as you cut.

TIP

Why not use up a bunch of different scraps rather than just cutting red and yellow rectangles? You can cut them out from different fabrics.

CUTTING

Fabric A (ivory)

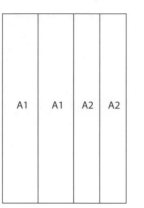

1. Cut 2 strips 7½" × WOF (selvage to selvage) and sew end to end; trim A1.

2. Cut 2 strips 5½" × WOF and sew end to end; trim A2.

   A1: 7½" × 60"   **A2:** 5½" × 60"

Fabric B (black)

B1, B2, B3, B4, B5, & B6

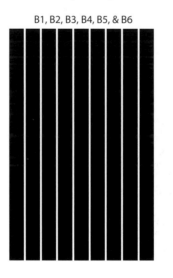

Cut 9 strips 2½" × WOF; sew groups of 3 strips end to end. Trim B1, B2, B3, B4, B5, and B6.

   B1, B2, B3, B4, B5, and B6: 2½" × 60"

Fabric C (gold)

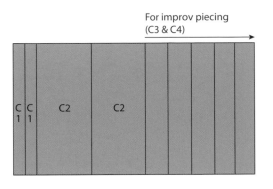

For improv piecing
(C3 & C4) →

1. Cut 2 strips 3½″ × WOF and sew end to end; trim C1.

2. Cut 2 strips 16½″ × WOF and sew end to end; trim C2.

3. Cut 3 strips 7″ × WOF for C3.

4. Cut 1 strip 6″ × WOF for C4.

C1: 3½″ × 60″   C3: 7″ × WOF (3 strips)

C2: 16½ × 60″   C4: 6″ × WOF

Fabric D (red)

1. Cut 6–8 rectangles 2½″–3½″ × 6″.

2. Cut 12–15 rectangles 2½″–3½″ × 7″.

Fabric E (yellow)

1. Cut 1 rectangle 2½″–3½″ × 6″.

2. Cut 1 rectangle 2½″–3½″ × 7″.

Assembling the Quilt Top

Press after each step.

MAKING THE IMPROV STRIPES

1. Trim off a piece of C3 and sew a 7″ Fabric D rectangle to one side of C3. Sew the remainder of the C3 strip to the other side of the Fabric D rectangle; trim to a random length. Add another 7″ D rectangle. Continue in this manner until the stripe is 60″ long. Trim, if necessary.

2. Trim the stripe to 6½″ × 60″ (Stripe 1).

3. Repeat Steps 1 and 2 to make Stripe 3, but this time replace 1 red rectangle with the 7″ Fabric E rectangle.

4. Trim off a piece of C4 and sew a 6″ Fabric D rectangle to one side of it. Sew the remainder of the C4 strip to the other side of the Fabric D rectangle; trim again, randomly. Add another 6″ D rectangle. Continue in this manner until the stripe is 60″ long (be sure to add the 6″ Fabric E rectangle somewhere). Trim, if necessary.

TIP

If you run short of C4, use some of what's left of the second C3 strip to fill in.

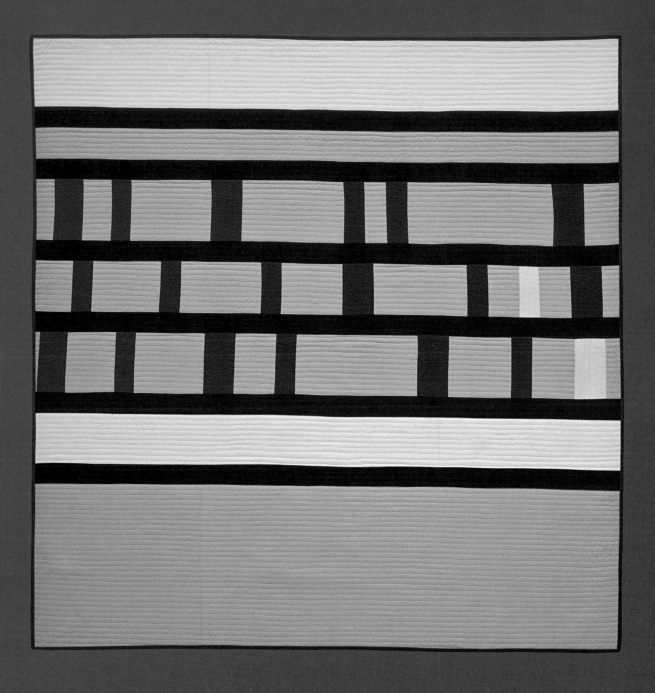

5. Trim to 5½″ × 60″ (Stripe 2).

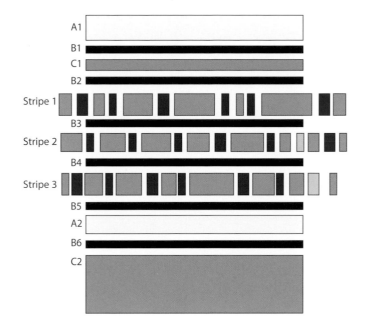

6. Assemble the quilt top by sewing A1, B1, C1, B2, Stripe 1, B3, Stripe 2, B4, Stripe 3, B5, A2, B6, and C2 to each other, in that order.

Making the Quilt Back

To make a 70″ × 70″ quilt back, cut 2 pieces 70″ × WOF and remove the selvages. Sew the 2 pieces together along the 70″ edges. Trim to 70″ long.

Quilting Options

OPTION 1

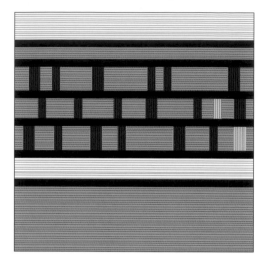

OPTION 2

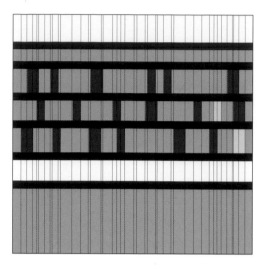

The allover dense straight-line quilting on this quilt can take some time to complete, but it is worth the extra effort. For all of this quilting, I used thread colors that matched the fabric.

I started by turning the quilt 90° (on its side) so that I could quilt straight horizontal lines across the width of the quilt. Starting with the center-most black stripe and working to the right, I used matching thread to quilt the straight lines that run across the entire width of the quilt. Once I got to the outside edge, I rotated the quilt 180° and worked my way out from the next center-most black stripe in the same manner.

I then rotated the quilt back 90° and filled in the red and yellow rectangles with vertical lines. Then I rotated the quilt 90° again and filled in the gold gaps between the rectangles. As I stopped and started on each side of the rectangles, I sewed locking stitches. Then I trimmed off all the running threads.

Another option that keeps the stark, graphic feel to the quilt is to fill in with vertical straight lines. Each line runs along the outside edge of one of the rectangles in the 3 rows. Add 2 more lines down the center of the quilt to fill it in thoroughly. With a walking foot, start in the middle of the quilt and work your way out to the right. When you're done with the first half, rotate the quilt 180° and repeat the process on the other side.

MONOCHROMATIC QUILTS

MUSTARD

60" × 70"

CUTTING

Fabric A (pale yellow)

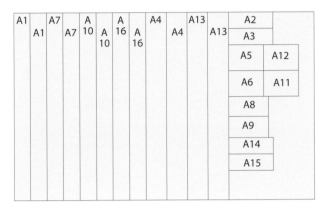

1. Cut 8 strips 3½" × WOF (selvage to selvage) and sew in pairs end to end to make 4 strips; trim A1, A7, A10, and A16.

2. Cut 4 strips 4½" × WOF and sew in 2 pairs end to end; trim A4 and A13.

3. Cut A2, A3, A5, A6, A8, A9, A11, A12, A14, and A15.

A1: 3½" × 70½"	A7: 3½" × 70½"	A13: 4½" × 70½"
A2: 9½" × 3½"	A8: 8½" × 4½"	A14: 9½" × 3½"
A3: 9½" × 3½"	A9: 8½" × 4½"	A15: 9½" × 3½"
A4: 4½" × 70½"	A10: 3½" × 70½"	A16: 3½" × 70½"
A5: 7½" × 5½"	A11: 7½" × 5½"	
A6: 7½" × 5½"	A12: 7½" × 5½"	

This bright, elegant throw consists of large, simple rectangles.

Although there aren't many pieces to sew together, attentive cutting and piecing are key for this pattern to align properly. Be sure to measure twice and cut once with this one!

WHAT YOU NEED

Based on 42" fabric width.

Fabric A (pale yellow): 2⅛ yards for background

Fabric B (light yellow): 1¼ yards

Fabric C (medium yellow): 1⅛ yards

Fabric D (dark yellow): ¾ yard

Fabric E (yellow print): 5½" × 7½" (optional)

Backing: 4¼ yards

Binding: ¾ yard

Please be sure to read Notes on *Making the Quilts in This Book* (page 6). Label the pieces as you cut.

MODERN MINIMAL

Cutting, continued

Fabric B (light yellow)

Cut 4 strips 9½" × WOF and sew in pairs end to end to make 2 strips; trim B1 and B2.

> B1: 9½" × 64½"
>
> B2: 9½" × 64½"

Fabric C (medium yellow)

Cut 4 strips 7½" × WOF and sew in pairs end to end to make 2 strips; trim C1 and C2.

> C1: 60½" × 7½"
>
> C2: 60½" × 7½"

If you would like to include Fabric E, it is pieced into C1 at the location of your choice. Trim the resulting strip to 60½".

Fabric D (dark yellow)

Cut 2 strips 8½" × WOF and sew end to end; trim D1.

> D1: 8½" × 62½"

Fabric E (optional yellow print)

> E1: This piece is already cut to size.

Assembling the Quilt Top

Press after each step.

Accurate cutting and piecing are important for everything to match up correctly. Before you assemble the fabric strips with the background fabric, be sure to lay them out to make sure they line up correctly.

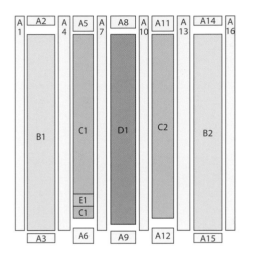

As you sew together the long seams, be sure to pin all along the length of the fabric thoroughly. Backstitch at the beginnings and ends of the seams.

Making the Quilt Back

To make a 70" × 80" quilt back, cut 2 pieces 70" × WOF and remove the selvages. Sew the 2 pieces together along the 70" edges.

Quilting Options

OPTION 1

OPTION 2

I stitched a straight-line quilting pattern to stay in keeping with the design's graphic nature.

First, I quilted the big rectangular spirals in the columns, starting with the center column. I began on the outside edge of each column and slowly worked my way into the center. I had to take care that the fabric in the column was very smooth, so I didn't end up with a bubble of fabric in the center of the column.

I filled in the same type of rectangular spiral in the remaining columns, working out from the center of the quilt. When I finished with the spirals, I sewed vertical lines through all the vertical background strips. I finished the quilting by sewing 2 horizontal lines of quilting across the top and bottom edges of the quilt.

Alternately, you could quilt in a straight-line pattern of shallow V's. Using chalk or a marking pen, draw on the first of the V's. Using a quilting bar to keep the lines equidistant, rotate the quilt 90° and fill in half of the shallow V's. Then, rotate the quilt 180° and fill in the opposite side. Once the longer V's are all quilted, fill in the central portions of the quilt by echoing smaller V's.

This quilt will fit a full bed—or a twin bed with a lot of overhang. A quilt this big is always great to have around the living room to wrap up in while watching a movie.

The most basic of designs, this pattern simply involves sewing together long vertical strips in varying widths. The gradual decrease in size of the dark green strips creates the illusion of a curve.

WHAT YOU NEED

Based on 42" fabric width.

Fabric A (dark green): 3¾ yards

Fabric B (light green): 1⅝ yards

Fabric C (optional yellow print): 21½" × 10½"

Backing: 5⅝ yards

Binding: ⅞ yard

Please be sure to read Notes on Making the Quilts in This Book (page 6). Label the pieces as you cut.

CUTTING

> **TIP** If you find it easier, don't trim your strips to 80". You can piece the entire quilt top using the extra-long strips, and then trim the top to 80".

Fabric A (dark green)

1. Cut 2 strips 21½" × WOF (selvage to selvage) and sew end to end; trim A1.

2. Cut 2 strips 16½" × WOF and sew end to end; trim A2.

3. Cut 2 strips 10½" × WOF and sew end to end; trim A3.

4. Cut 2 strips 6½" × WOF and sew end to end; trim A4.

5. Cut 2 strips 4½" × WOF and sew end to end; trim A5.

6. Cut 2 strips 2½" × WOF and sew end to end; trim A6.

7. Cut 2 strips 1½" × WOF and sew end to end; trim A7.

A1: 21½" × 80"	A4: 6½" × 80"	A7: 1½" × 80"
A2: 16½" × 80"	A5: 4½" × 80"	
A3: 10½" × 80"	A6: 2½" × 80"	

Fabric B (light green)

Cut 16 strips 2½" × WOF and sew in pairs end to end to make 8 strips; trim to 80".

B: 8 strips 2½" × 80"

If you would like to include the optional yellow print, it is pieced into the second B strip at the location of your choice. Trim the resulting strip to 80".

Assembling the Quilt Top

Press after each step.

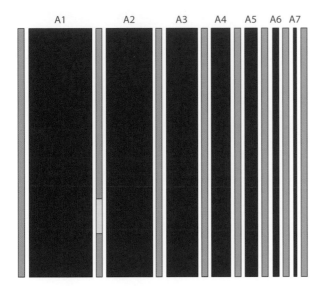

With seams this long, pinning is crucial. Remember to backstitch at the beginning and end of each seam. Assemble the quilt as shown. Trim to square up.

Making the Quilt Back

To make an 86″ × 90″ quilt back, cut 2 pieces 86″ × WOF and remove the selvages. Sew the 2 pieces together along the 86″ edges. Then add 6″ more to the bottom as follows: Cut 3 strips 6½″ × WOF, piece them together, trim to 86″, and sew the long strip to the bottom of the quilt back.

Quilting Options

OPTION 1

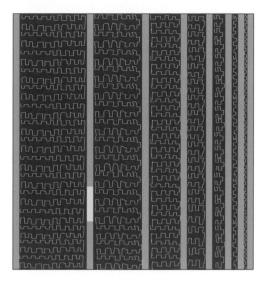

I wanted to keep the light green lines on this quilt a bit raised compared to the dark green, so I only quilted the dark green areas of the quilt. I filled in each dark green area with a boxy free-motion pattern.

I started at the top of the center dark green panel and filled in the quilt with rows of the pattern, working my way down the panel, row after row. I continued filling in the quilt, dark green panel after dark green panel, working my way to the right from the center. When I finished that half of the quilt, I rotated the quilt 180° and worked my way out from the center again.

OPTION 2

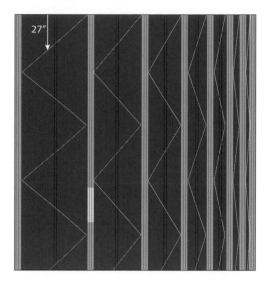

Another choice is to fill in each dark green area of the quilt with a large zigzag. If you need to, mark the initial zig at the top of each dark green strip. This measures 27″ long in all strips but angles differently in each one, narrowing with each narrower strip of the quilt. After each area is filled in with a zigzag, add 2 straight lines of stitching that run through the center of each dark green strip and through all the light green strips.

CUTTING

Please be sure to read Notes on Making the Quilts in This Book (page 6). Label the pieces as you cut.

When cutting out the fabrics, you'll cut out rectangles that will then be trimmed after being sewn to the growing center of the quilt top. These measurements worked very well when I made this quilt ... twice! But different people are likely to cut that 5° angle differently and so, if you would rather be safe, stitch on the rounds of strips and then trim them to size instead of cutting the strips to size first.

Fabric A (lightest red)

Cut 1 rectangle 5½″ × 10½″.

A: 5½″ × 10½″

Fabric B

Cut 2 strips 4½″ × WOF (selvage to selvage); trim B1, B2, B3, and B4.

B1: 4½″ × 10½″   B3: 4½″ × 13½″

B2: 4½″ × 10½″   B4: 4½″ × 13½″

Fabric C

1. Cut 1 strip 4½″ × WOF; trim C1 and C3.

2. Cut 1 strip 4½″ × WOF; trim C2 and C4.

C1: 4½″ × 17½″   C3: 4½″ × 20½″

C2: 4½″ × 17½″   C4: 4½″ × 20½″

Fabric D

Cut 4 strips 5½″ × WOF; trim D1, D2, D3, and D4.

D1: 5½″ × 24″   D3: 5½″ × 28″

D2: 5½″ × 24″   D4: 5½″ × 28″

This small throw is made up of six different shades of red solids that range from light to dark. The range of colors creates an optical illusion of depth.

When making this quilt, picking the right grouping of fabrics is key in order to duplicate the gradual color graduation. When picking fabrics like this, I tend to stack them up and slightly blur my eyes as I look at them. This helps me see if one fabric "pops" in a way that I don't like. This pop often means that a fabric has the wrong value. Even if it seems to be the right color, sometimes it is too saturated when placed next to the other fabrics.

This quilt top is made by cutting the framing strips as rectangles and then trimming them to create the off-kilter framing.

WHAT YOU NEED

Based on 42″ fabric width.

Fabric A (red 1*): 5½″ × 10½″

Fabric B (red 2*): ½ yard

Fabric C (red 3*): ½ yard

Fabric D (red 4*): ¾ yard

Fabric E (red 5*): 1 yard

Fabric F (red 6*): 1¾ yards

Backing: 3⅝ yards

Binding: ¾ yard

* Use 6 shades of red, from 1 (lightest) to 6 (darkest)—coral, red, rich red, wine, crimson, and burgundy are the names of the Kona cottons I used.

Fabric E

Cut 4 strips 6½" × WOF; trim E1, E2, E3, and E4.

E1: 6½" × 31"   E3: 6½" × 36"

E2: 6½" × 31"   E4: 6½" × 36"

Fabric F (darkest red)

1. Cut 5 strips 10½" × WOF.

2. From 2 of the strips from Step 1, trim F1 and F2.

3. Cut 2 pieces 10½" × 10½" from a WOF strip from Step 1.

4. Sew these to the ends of the 2 remaining WOF strips; trim F2 and F3.

F1: 10½" × 40½"   F3: 10½" × 50½"

F2: 10½" × 40½"   F3: 10½" × 50½"

Assembling the Quilt Top

Press after each step.

1. Sew B1 and B2 to opposite sides of A.

2. Add B3 and B4 to the top and bottom of this unit.

3. Trim a 5° angle off the left and right sides of your piecing using a protractor and a ruler. Trim the top and bottom square with the sides.

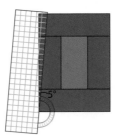

4. Sew C1 and C2 to the sides of this unit; sew C3 and C4 to the top and bottom.

5. Again you'll trim all 4 sides, but this time at the opposite 5° angle.

6. Repeat Steps 4 and 5 to add Fabric D. Remember to reverse the angle that you use to trim the sides.

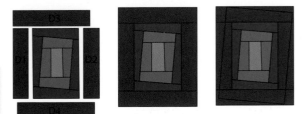

TIP

If you don't happen to still have your high school protractor, find one online, download it, print it on cardstock, and cut it out.

7. Repeat the process to add Fabric E, again reversing the trim angle.

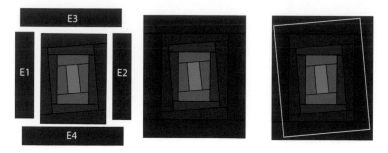

8. Sew F1 and F2 to the sides and sew F3 and F4 to the top and bottom of the quilt top.

9. Square up to 50½" × 60½" and your top is complete.

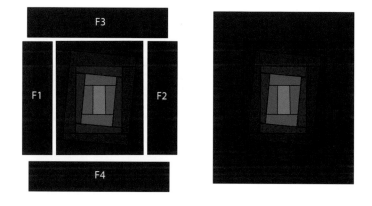

The more rounds you sew on the quilt, the harder it will be to trim, because the lines you're cutting are longer and longer. I used chalk and a ruler to draw the line to make certain that I cut an accurate straight line, even if I had to stop trimming halfway through to adjust my ruler and quilt top.

Making the Quilt Back

To make a 60" × 70" quilt back, cut 2 pieces 60" × WOF and remove the selvages. Sew the 2 pieces together along the 60" edges. Trim to 70".

Quilting Options

OPTION 1

OPTION 2

To keep the sense of depth in this design while also drawing attention to the off-kilter wonky piecing, I quilted a huge square spiral all over the face of the quilt.

I started in the middle and used a walking foot. I kept the space between each "round" of the spiral relatively even. I didn't measure this at all; I just kept an eye on it as I worked my way around. I also took the time to match the thread to each shade of red as I reached each new round of fabric. See a close-up of the actual quilting (page 135).

Another option is to quilt along all the piecing lines but carry each quilting line all along the entire length of the quilt. With a walking foot, start with the center-most rectangle in the quilt and quilt straight lines that run right along the piecing lines. If it helps, use a ruler and a marking pen to mark the lines. Repeat with all the rounds of red in the quilt.

CHOPPY WATERS | 65" × 87"

CUTTING

TIP If you find it easier, don't trim the strips to 65″. Instead, piece the entire quilt top using the extra-long strips, and then trim it to 65″.

Fabric A

1. Cut 2 strips 4½″ × WOF (selvage to selvage) and sew end to end; trim A1.

2. Cut 2 strips 3½″ × WOF and sew end to end; trim A2.

3. Cut 2 strips 7½″ × WOF and sew end to end; trim A3.

A1: 4½″ × 65″   A2: 3½″ × 65″   A3: 7½″ × 65″

If you would like to include the optional blue print, it is pieced into A2 at the location of your choice. Trim resulting strip to 65″.

Blue print

This piece has already been cut to size.

Fabric B

1. Cut 2 strips 7½″ × WOF and sew end to end; trim B1.

2. Cut 2 strips 4½″ × WOF and sew end to end; trim B2.

3. Cut 2 strips 3½″ × WOF and sew end to end; trim B3.

B1: 7½″ × 65″   B2: 4½″ × 65″   B3: 3½″ × 65″

Fabric C

1. Cut 2 strips 3½″ × WOF and sew end to end; trim C1.

2. Cut 2 strips 4½″ × WOF and sew end to end; trim C2.

3. Cut 2 strips 8½″ × WOF and sew end to end; trim C3.

4. Cut 2 strips 3½″ × WOF and sew end to end; trim C4.

C1: 3½″ × 65″   C3: 8½″ × 65″

C2: 4½″ × 65″   C4: 3½″ × 65″

This twin-size quilt is made from six shades of blue fabrics. A random mix of strips in different colors and sizes, the simple design has a surprising amount of movement because of the different color tones.

The quilt comes together very easily. Feel free to mix up the order in which you piece the strips. This pattern is straightforward, so put your own spin on it!

WHAT YOU NEED

Based on 42″ fabric width.

Fabric A: 1⅛ yards

Blue print: 3½″ × 11″ *(optional)*

Fabric B: 1⅛ yards

Fabric C: 1⅜ yards

Fabric D: ⅞ yard

Fabric E: 1¼ yards

Fabric F: 1¼ yards

Backing: 5¼ yards

Binding: ⅞ yard

Note

Choose 6 shades of blue— any that you think are pretty together. As long as there is variety in their tones, they will work.

Please be sure to read Notes on Making the Quilts in This Book (page 6). Label the pieces as you cut.

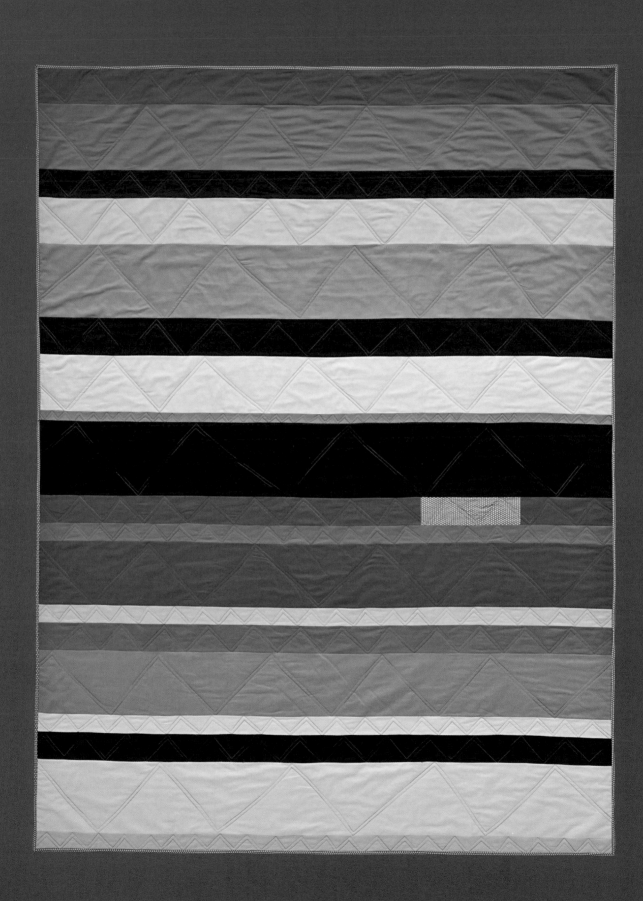

Cutting, continued

Fabric D

1. Cut 2 strips 5½" × WOF and sew end to end; trim D1.

2. Cut 2 strips 2½" × WOF and sew end to end; trim D2.

3. Cut 2 strips 2½" × WOF and sew end to end; trim D3.

D1: 5½" × 65"   D3: 2½" × 65"

D2: 2½" × 65"

Fabric E

1. Cut 2 strips 8½" × WOF and sew end to end; trim E1.

2. Cut 2 strips 1½" × WOF and sew end to end; trim E2.

3. Cut 2 strips 7½" × WOF and sew end to end; trim E3.

E1: 8½" × 65"   E3: 7½" × 65"

E2: 1½" × 65"

Fabric F

1. Cut 2 strips 6½" × WOF and sew end to end; trim F1.

2. Cut 2 strips 2½" × WOF and sew end to end; trim F2.

3. Cut 2 strips 8½" × WOF and sew end to end; trim F3.

F1: 6½" × 65"   F3: 8½" × 65"

F2: 2½" × 65"

Assembling the Quilt Top

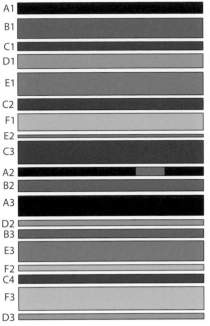

Press after each step.

1. If you are going to add the optional blue print, piece it into A2 now and trim to 65".

2. Sew the strips as shown. With seams this long, be sure to pin extensively so you can just sew along the entire seam quickly and evenly with a nice straight seam allowance. Remember to backstitch at the beginning and end of each seam. Trim to square up.

TIP

- So that you don't end up with seams from the pieced stripes lining up across the quilt top, alternate which end of the strip the seam is on as you sew the strips.

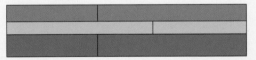

- You might prefer to piece the top in sections. First, sew together the stripes in pairs, then all of the pairs into fours, and so on. It's more of a challenge to keep track of what goes where, but in this quilt the order of the stripes doesn't really matter as long as you don't have two same-color stripes next to each other.

Making the Quilt Back

To make a 75" × 97" quilt back, cut 2 pieces 75" × WOF and remove the selvages. Sew the 2 pieces together along the 75" edges. Then add 13" more to the bottom as follows: Cut 2 strips 13½" × WOF, piece them together, trim to 75", and sew the long strip to the bottom of the quilt back.

Quilting Options

OPTION 1

OPTION 2

For this quilt, I zigzagged within the width of each stripe. For each zig and zag, I took care to turn a nice 45° angle. If it helps, keep a ruler on hand so you can use its corner to make sure your turns are 45°.

Starting with the center stripe, I rotated the quilt on its side. Using a walking foot, I sewed a zigzag on each stripe, making sure that at the top of each stripe I left enough space for the second echoed line of quilting.

When I finished one side, I rotated the quilt 180° and worked my way out from the center through the other half of the quilt. Then, I repeated the entire process, adding the second line of echo quilting. See a close-up of the actual quilting (page 140).

This incredibly basic quilting pattern creates a great graphic contrast to all the horizontal stripes in the piecing. Simply quilt repeats of 4 dense lines from top to bottom, leaving 4″ or 5″ spaces between them. Work your way from the center out to the right and then rotate the quilt 180° and repeat that process.

BABY QUILTS

DON'T FENCE ME IN | 45" × 60"

CUTTING

Fabric A (pink)

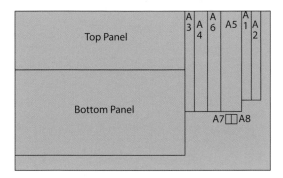

1. Cut 1 piece 45½" × WOF (selvage to selvage).

2. From the piece in Step 1, cut 15½" × 45½" parallel to the selvage for the top panel.

3. From the piece in Step 1, cut 22½" × 45½" parallel to the selvage for the bottom panel.

4. Cut 2 strips 3" × WOF; trim A1 and A2.

5. Cut 1 strip 2½" × WOF; trim A3.

6. Cut 1 strip 3½" × WOF; trim A4.

7. Cut 1 strip 5½" × WOF; trim A5.

8. Cut 1 strip 3½" × WOF; trim A6.

9. Trim A7 and A8 from scraps.

Top panel: 15½" × 45½"	A1: 3" × 23½"	A5: 5½" × 26½"
	A2: 3" × 23½"	A6: 3½" × 26½"
Bottom panel: 22½" × 45½"	A3: 2½" × 26½"	A7: 1½" × 3½"
	A4: 3½" × 26½"	A8: 1½" × 3½"

This cute little quilt is perfect for your friends' baby girls! I always tend to make my baby quilts this size. It's a bit big for a crib, but it means that a baby will cuddle under this cozy quilt well into her toddler years.

This quilt uses strip piecing. To create the fence, first we'll sew together strips and cut up that piecing; then we'll sew it to additional strips.

WHAT YOU NEED

Based on 42" fabric width.

Fabric A (pink): 2⅛ yards for background

Fabric B (gray): ¾ yard

Fabric C (white): ½ yard

Backing: 3⅓ yards

Binding: ¾ yard

Please be sure to read Notes on Making the Quilts in This Book (page 6). Label the pieces as you cut.

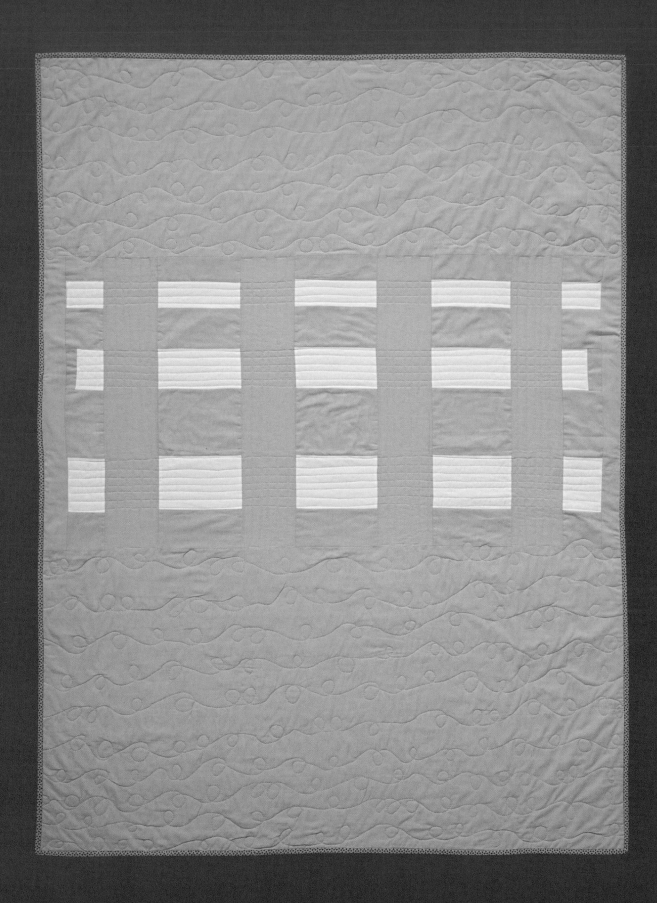

Fabric B (gray)

Cut an 18″ × 23½″ rectangle; subcut it into 4 strips 4½″ × 23½″.

> B1: 4½″ × 23½″ (4 strips)

Fabric C (white)

1. Cut a 7″ × 26½″ rectangle; trim C1 and C3.
2. Cut 1 strip 3½″ × 24½″; trim C2.

> C1: 2½″ × 26½″   C3: 5½″ × 26½″
>
> C2: 3½″ × 24½″

Assembling the Quilt Top

Press after each step.

1. Sew A7 and A8 to opposite ends of C2.

A7 ─ | C2 | ─ A8

2. Sew A3, C1, A4, A7/C2/A8, A5, C3, and A6.

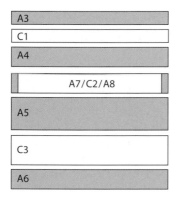

3. Cut the strip set into columns 1 through 5 that measure 3½″, 6½″, 6½″, 6½″, and 3½″ wide, respectively.

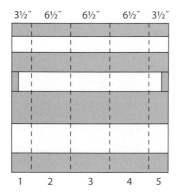

4. Working left to right, assemble the fence panel.

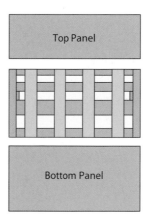

5. Add the top and bottom panels to the central fence panel and you are all finished with your quilt top.

Top Panel

(central fence panel)

Bottom Panel

Making the Quilt Back

To make a 55″ × 70″ quilt back, cut 2 pieces 55″ × WOF and remove the selvages. Sew the 2 pieces together along the 55″ edges. Trim to 70″.

Quilting Options

OPTION 1

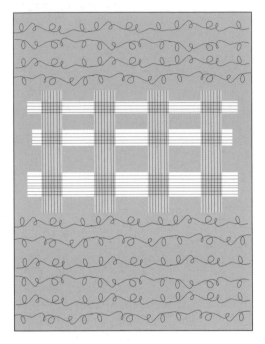

OPTION 2

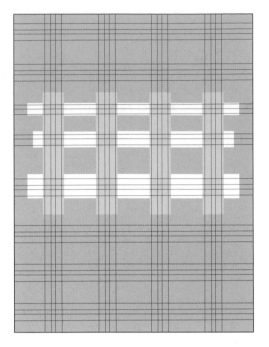

I emphasized the piecing on the quilt top by sewing vertical and horizontal lines to match the gray and white "fence" piecing. Then I free-motion quilted whimsical curlicues in rows along the open space of the quilt's top and bottom.

First, I quilted enough dense lines (using the edge of my walking foot as a guide) to fill each strip of gray or white. I sewed all the horizontal lines first and then the vertical lines. Then I switched to a free-motion foot. I turned the quilt on its side. Starting at the center, I worked out and sewed rows of curlicues. Once I reached the edge, I rotated the quilt 180° and repeated this process to fill in the other side. See a close-up of the actual quilting (page 137).

Another way to quilt this design is to fill it with a simple plaid pattern that mirrors the fence. Use a walking foot to fill in the set of 3 vertical lines. Then turn the quilt on its side and repeat with the horizontal lines. Take care that both the vertical and horizontal lines run right through the fence.

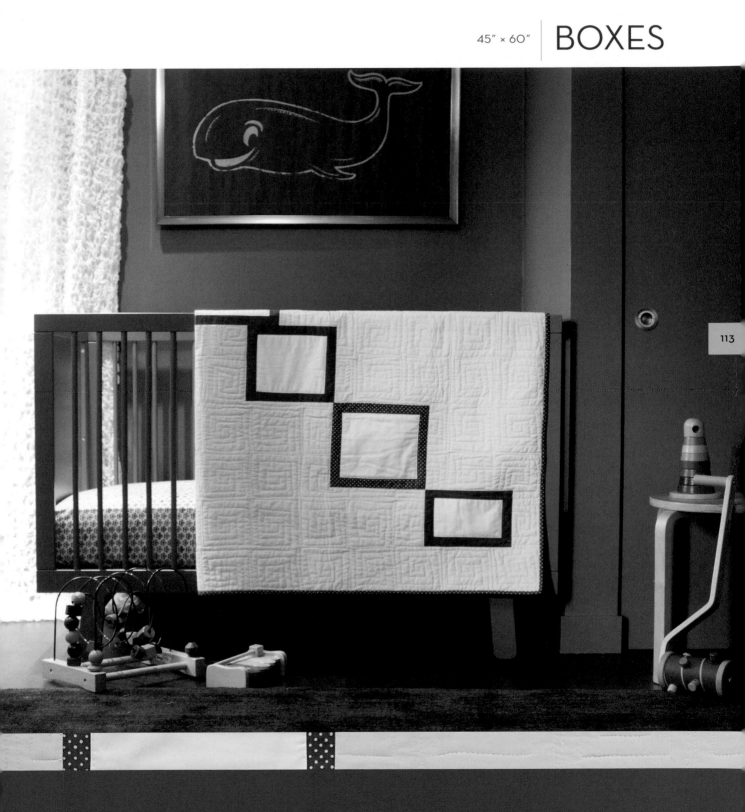

113

This cute baby quilt with a boxy pattern will be loved by both parent and child. A simple graphic pattern like this goes well in any modern and cool nursery.

I chose to frame one of the boxes in a polka dot brown fabric. I thought this pattern would add a bit of interest and youthfulness to the baby quilt. Feel free to frame any or all of the boxes in a different fabric!

WHAT YOU NEED

Based on 42" fabric width.

Fabric A (blue): 2¼ yards for background

Fabric B (brown): ¼ yard

Fabric C (ivory): ½ yard

Fabric D (brown print): 1½" × WOF (selvage to selvage)

Backing: 3⅓ yards

Binding: ¾ yard

Please be sure to read Notes on Making the Quilts in This Book (page 6). Label the pieces as you cut.

CUTTING

Fabric A (blue)

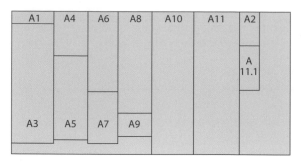

1. Cut 1 strip 11½" × WOF; trim A1 and A3.

2. Cut 1 strip 9½" × WOF; trim A4 and A5.

3. Cut 1 strip 8½" × WOF; trim A6 and A7.

4. Cut 1 strip 9½" × WOF; trim A8 and A9.

5. Cut 1 strip 11½" × WOF; trim A10.

6. Cut 1 strip 12½" × WOF; cut and sew a 6" × 12½" scrap to the strip; trim A11.

7. Cut A2.

A1: 3½" × 11½"	**A5:** 9½" × 23½"	**A9:** 6½" × 9½"
A2: 5½" × 9½"	**A6:** 8½" × 22½"	**A10:** 11½" × 40½"
A3: 11½" × 33½"	**A7:** 8½" × 14½"	**A11:** 12½" × 45½"
A4: 9½" × 12½"	**A8:** 9½" × 28½"	

Fabric B (brown)

Cut 4 strips 1½" × WOF.

Fabric C (ivory)

Cut 1 strip 9½" × WOF; trim C4 and C5. Trim the remainder of the strip to 7½" wide; trim C1, C2, and C3.

C1: 7½" × 4½"	**C3:** 6½" × 7½"	**C5:** 4½" × 9½"
C2: 7½" × 8½"	**C4:** 7½" × 9½"	

Fabric D (brown print)

Cut 1 strip 1½" × WOF.

Assembling the Quilt Top

Press after each step.

1. Sew Fabric B to one side of C1 and trim. Sew Fabric B to the opposite side of C1 and trim. Repeat this process to add Fabric B to the other 2 sides of C1.

2. Repeat Step 1 for C3 and C4.

3. Repeat Step 1 using Fabric D for C2.

4. For C5, add Fabric B to only the left side, top, and bottom.

Row 1 — A1, A2, A3, C1
Row 2 — A4, C2, A5
Row 3 — A6, C3, A7
Row 4 — A8, C4, A9
Row 5 — A10, C5
A11, A 11.1

5. Once all the boxes are framed, assemble the quilt top as shown.

Making the Quilt Back

To make a 55″ × 70″ quilt back, cut 2 pieces 55″ × WOF and remove the selvages. Sew the 2 pieces together along the 55″ edges. Trim to 70″.

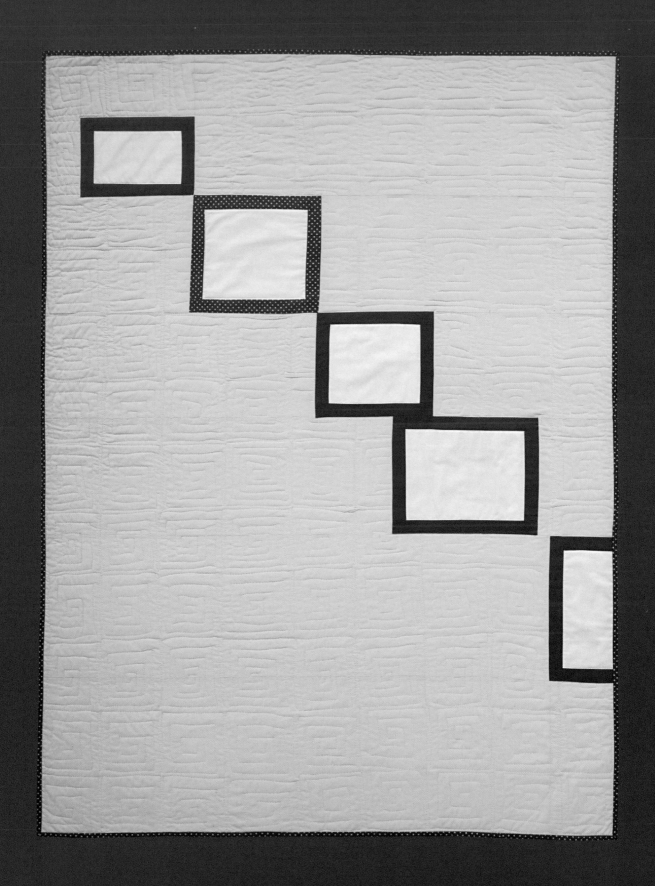

Quilting Options

OPTION 1

OPTION 2

I wanted to continue the boxes theme in the quilting, so I covered the negative space with an allover free-motion pattern of a grid of square spirals.

First, I used the walking foot to echo quilt the inside of the white rectangles and the outside of the brown framing. Then I pinned the quilt to a wall and used chalk to draw a 5″ grid all over the quilt. If any boxes were in the way of the grid, I drew the partial lines that would show.

Using a free-motion foot, I filled in each box with a square spiral, working in rows from the center out across the quilt and pushing out any excess fabric as I went. If a box was in the way of the grid, I filled in the portion of the spiral that was showing.

A different approach to the quilting is to fill the quilt with a zigzag straight-line quilting pattern that mirrors the boxes. First, with a walking foot, fill in the initial zigzags that follow each side of the boxes. Then, echo quilt those seams, first filling out one side and then the other side of the quilt. Use a quilting bar to keep the seams equidistant. How densely you fill the lines is up to you, but keep them no more than 2″ apart.

BUILDING BLOCKS | 30″ × 43″

Please be sure to read Notes on Making the Quilts in This Book (page 6). Label the pieces as you cut.

CUTTING

Fabric A (gray)

1. Cut 1 strip 9½" × WOF (selvage to selvage); trim A1, A3, A5, A8, and A10.

2. Cut 1 strip 9½" × WOF and add the remaining fabric from Step 1; trim A11.

3. Trim the remainder of the strip from Step 2 to 6½" wide; trim A2, A4, A6, A7, and A9.

4. Cut 2 strips 2½" × WOF; trim A13, A14, A15, and A16.

Be the hit of the baby shower with this play mat that can be sewn up in no time flat.

This quilt takes very little yardage, and it doesn't require any pieces larger than 1⅛ yards, except for the backing. For a more eclectic look, try using a different fabric for every block. Large-scale patterned fabric works well for this quilt, since relatively large pieces of fabric are used for each "block."

WHAT YOU NEED

Based on 42" fabric width.

Fabric A (gray): 1⅛ yards

Fabric B (blue 1): 2 rectangles 11½" × 10½"

Fabric C (blue 2): 1 rectangle 11½" × 10½"

Fabric D (green 1*): 1 rectangle 6½" × 7½"

Fabric E (green 2*): 1 rectangle 6½" × 7½"

Fabric F (green 3*): 1 rectangle 6½" × 7½"

Fabric G (green 4*): 1 rectangle 6½" × 7½"

Backing: 1⅔ yards

Binding: ⅝ yard

* I used 3 different green solids and a green print.

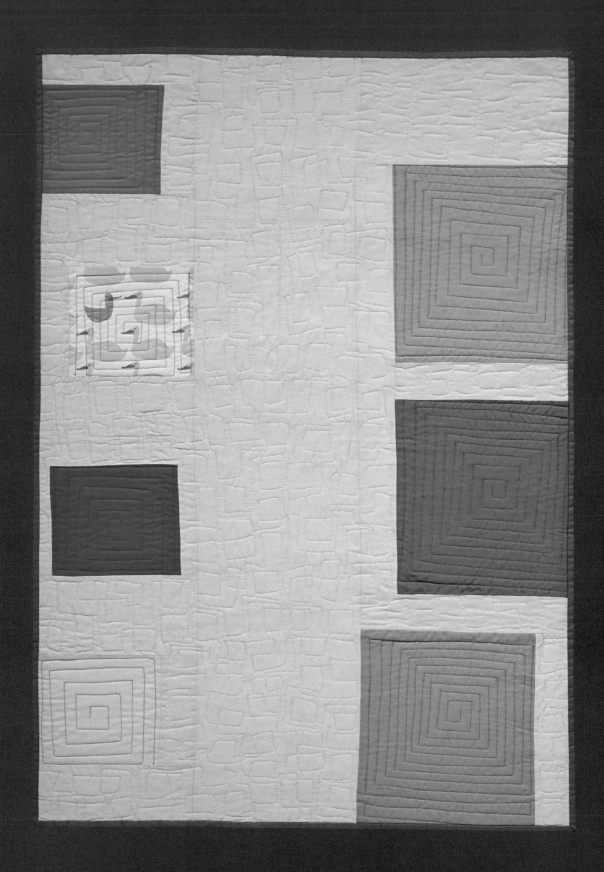

Cutting, continued

5. Cut 1 rectangle
6½″ × 12½″ for A12.

A1: 2½″ × 9½″

A2: 2½″ × 6½″

A3: 4½″ × 9½″

A4: 2½″ × 6½″

A5: 5½″ × 9½″

A6: 1½″ × 6½″

A7: 1½″ × 6½″

A8: 5″ × 9½″

A9: 2½″ × 6½″

A10: 4″ × 9½″

A11: 9½″ × 43½″

A12: 6½″ × 12½″

A13: 2½″ × 24½″

A14: 2½″ × 10½″

A15: 2½″ × 12½″

A16: 2½″ × 11½″

Assembling the Quilt Top

Press after each step.

1. Sew Green 1 to A2, A4 to Green 2, A6 and A7 to Green 3, Green 4 to A9, Blue 1 and Blue 2 to A14, and the second Blue 1 to A16.

2. Sew the Blue 1 / A14 / Blue 2 unit to A13.

3. Sew the first column together: A1 to Green 1 / A2, then add A3 to A4 / Green 2 and so on.

4. Sew A12 to the top of the A13 / Blue 1 / A14 / Blue 2 unit. Sew A15 to the bottom of that strip. Sew Blue 1 / A16 to the bottom of that.

5. Sew the units from Step 3 and Step 4 to opposite sides of A11.

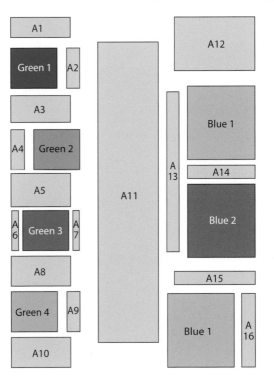

Making the Quilt Back

To make a 40″ × 53″ quilt back, cut the fabric 53″ long and remove the selvages.

Quilting Options

OPTION 1

OPTION 2

An allover boxy free-motion pattern gives this quilt great texture. First, I used a walking foot to fill in the green and blue boxes with a square spiral. Since this quilt is small, I could easily turn it through the machine as needed. Once I filled in all the boxes, I switched to a free-motion foot and filled in with an allover boxy meandering pattern that crossed over itself.

Another way to quilt this little play mat is to fill it with dense straight-line quilting that echoes the blocks. With a walking foot, first fill in around each block. From there, continue to echo the quilt and keep filling in with straight lines until you have filled in the entire quilt.

This baby quilt is filled with pretty pastels and mixes very traditional baby colors with an offbeat and asymmetrical pattern.

I have provided the exact measurements to duplicate this quilt, but feel free to mix it up and improv piece the columns as you'd like, making the design more your own.

WHAT YOU NEED

Based on 42" fabric width.

Fabric A (white): 1½ yards

Fabric B (pink): 1 yard

Fabric C (light green): ¼ yard

Fabric D (light blue): ¼ yard

Fabric E (light yellow): ¼ yard

Backing: 2½ yards

Binding: ⅝ yard

Please be sure to read Notes on Making the Quilts in This Book (page 6). Label the pieces as you cut.

CUTTING

Fabric A (white)

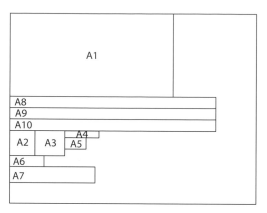

1. Cut 18½" parallel to the selvage; trim A1.

2. Cut 3 strips 2½" wide, parallel to the selvage; trim A8, A9, and A10.

3. Cut A2, A3, A4, A5, A6, and A7.

A1: 18½" × 35½"	A5: 2½" × 4½"	A9: 2½" × 45½"
A2: 5½" × 5½"	A6: 2½" × 7½"	A10: 2½" × 45½"
A3: 5½" × 6½"	A7: 3½" × 18½"	
A4: 1½" × 7½"	A8: 2½" × 45½"	

Fabric B (pink)

1. Cut 1 strip 7½" × WOF (selvage to selvage); trim B1, B2, B4, B5, B6, B8, B9, B11, B12, B14, and B16.

2. Cut 1 strip 7½" × WOF; trim B3, B7, B10, and B15.

3. Cut 1 strip 7½" × WOF; trim B13.

B1: 2½" × 7½"	B7: 10½" × 7½"	B13: 15½" × 7½"
B2: 4½" × 7½"	B8: 4½" × 7½"	B14: 2½" × 7½"
B3: 15½" × 7½"	B9: 4½" × 7½"	B15: 6½" × 7½"
B4: 1½" × 7½"	B10: 6½" × 7½"	B16: 2½" × 7½"
B5: 5½" × 7½"	B11: 2½" × 7½"	
B6: 2½" × 7½"	B12: 3½" × 7½"	

Fabric C (light green)

Cut 1 strip 5½" × WOF; trim 4 rectangles 5½" × 7½".

Fabric D (light blue)

Cut 1 strip 7½" × WOF; trim 6 rectangles 4½" × 7½".

Fabric E (light yellow)

Cut 1 strip 7½" × WOF; trim 7 rectangles 2½" × 7½".

Assembling the Quilt Top

Press after each step.

1. Sew A4 to D. Sew A2 to the left side and A3 to the right side of the sub-unit.

2. Sew A5 to the left of E and A6 to the right.

3. Sew the sub-unit from Step 2 to the bottom of the sub-unit from Step 1.

4. Sew A7 to the bottom of the sub-unit from Step 3.

5. Sew A1 to the top of the sub-unit from Step 4 to complete the left panel.

6. Sew Column 1 in order as shown in the diagram: B1 to C, C to D, D to B2, B2 to E, E to B3, B3 to C, C to B4, B4 to E, and E to B5.

7. In the same fashion, following the diagram, complete Columns 2 and 3.

8. Sew A8 to the right side of Column 1, sew A9 to the right side of Column 2, and sew A10 to the right side of Column 3.

9. Sew the sashed columns to each other in order as shown in the diagram.

10. Sew the joined columns to the sub-unit from Step 5.

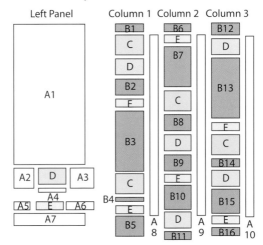

Making the Quilt Back

To make a 55" × 55" quilt back, cut 1 piece 55" × WOF and remove the selvages. Then add 13" more to the bottom as follows: Cut 2 strips 13½" × WOF, piece them together, trim to 55", and sew the long strip to the bottom of the quilt back.

Quilting Options

OPTION 1

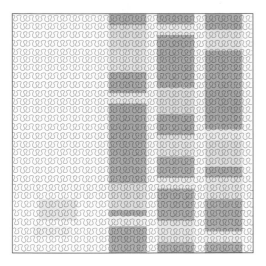

I added softness to this quilt by sewing allover rows of an easy rounded free-motion pattern.

I started at the top left corner and gradually worked my way across the quilt in rows. Because this quilt is small, it's easy to manage through a machine, even when you start all the way on one edge of the quilt.

OPTION 2

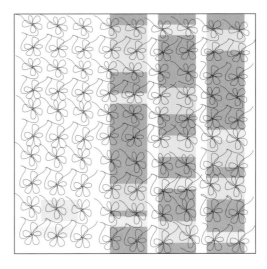

I think the girly nature of these colors lends itself a free-motion pattern that's rounded and soft. Develop a repeated flower pattern. On a scrap sandwich, practice the loops of a simple flower and then practice how you'll connect each flower to the next. When you are ready, start in the quilt center and quilt in rows (or columns, if working in that direction is easier for you) to fill the quilt with simple flowers.

HOW TO MAKE A QUILT

Tools

The primary tools used to cut fabric for quilting are a rotary cutter, an acrylic ruler, and a cutting mat. If you are new to quilting, these are some of the first tools you should buy. You can find them in affordable packs of all three at any good sewing store. You will use them all the time, and with a bit of practice, they will become second nature and invaluable to you.

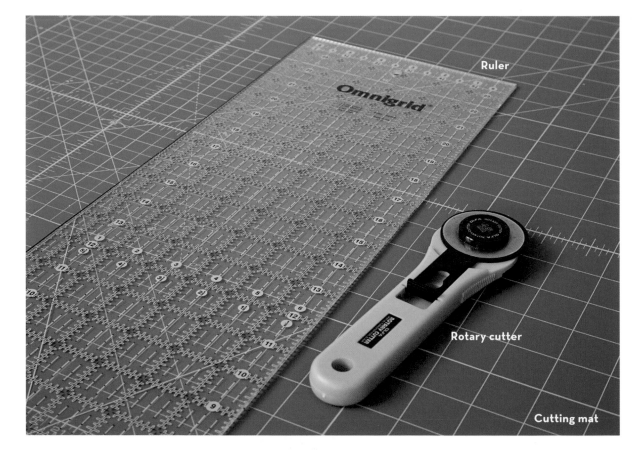

Ruler

Rotary cutter

Cutting mat

Rulers

Many different sizes of rulers are available. They can be expensive, so pick sizes that will serve more than one purpose. I find that the most useful ones are 6″ × 24″, 3″ × 18″, and 12½″ × 12½″.

Rotary Cutters

You can choose from a variety of rotary cutters. Choose one that you find comfortable to hold.

The blade in the cutter is very sharp, so be careful. Always cut away from yourself and be sure to keep your fingers away from the blade.

Remember to close the blade every time you stop cutting, even if you are only pausing for a moment. The rotary cutter will undoubtedly be knocked off your table or dropped on your fabric or your perfectly cut strips, and you want it to be closed when that happens.

Cutting Mat

Choose a mat that is large enough for you to work with various-sized pieces of fabric, preferably a mat that is 18″ × 24″ or larger. However, the mat should be small enough to fit on your workspace.

The cutting mat is covered with a grid. You will align everything you sew on this grid; you will then trim using the ruler. Get familiar with your mat, because you will be making hundreds and hundreds of cuts on it. Before long you will wrap your head around the ins and outs of using your ruler and mat grid to make straight cuts.

TIP

When you find yourself having to roll your rotary cutter over your fabric more than once, or if one roll isn't quite cutting through the fabric, it is time to replace the blade.

Piecing

Piecing is the term for sewing together the different pieces of fabric that build a quilt top. For all quilt patterns, the standard seam allowance is ¼". In quilting, it is important to master sewing a straight ¼" seam. Should your seam allowances be uneven or wavy, it will affect the quality of your piecing. Practice makes perfect.

If you are a beginning quilter, you might initially find sewing a straight ¼" seam a challenge. Consider purchasing a ¼" foot for your machine. You'll be amazed how much it will improve your accuracy. Practice until you can achieve an accurate ¼" seam allowance. It will make a huge difference in the success of your quilts.

Also consider adding a tape guide to your machine bed, adjacent to the presser foot. Place an acrylic ruler under the needle. With the power to your machine off, lower the needle manually to the ruler so that it lands precisely on the ¼" line. The ¼" should be to the right of the needle and the rest of the ruler to the left. Make sure the ruler is straight, and then lower the presser foot to hold it in place. Make a thick piece of tape by building up layers of tape or by using an X-Acto knife to cut through several layers at once with the tape still on the roll, and then place the thick tape on the machine bed alongside the ruler's edge. Place it closer to you and not exactly alongside the presser foot. This is especially helpful if you do not yet have a ¼" foot. Remove the ruler. This guide will help you to keep an accurate ¼" seam allowance.

If your machine has a ¼" foot, use it. If not, you might be able to buy one for your machine.

When sewing seams that will not be closed off with more piecing, backstitch at the beginning and end of the seam so that the seams don't separate as you baste and quilt the finished quilt top.

Improvisational Piecing

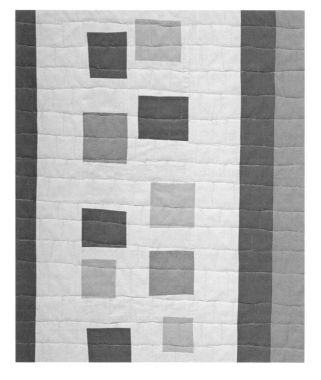

Often shortened to *improv piecing*, this type of piecing doesn't require specific measurements or cutting. Everything is done by eyeballing it and by using a cut-and-sew-as-you-go method. This technique makes for a creatively fulfilling process that is also very freeing. No two people's improv piecing is the same. The process of designing the quilt continues throughout the sewing of the quilt top, making the entire piecing process creatively enjoyable rather than simply being the labor of putting together a pattern, with no room for changes along the way.

This book contains a few patterns that include improv-pieced areas. Some people find tackling improv piecing daunting because there are no "rules" to follow. I find that doing some improv piecing in the context of a pattern can be easier to manage for a first improv project. It can be easy and enjoyable. So if you've never done improv piecing before, don't let it scare you off. The more you do it, the more you will find your own style and voice.

Pressing

Pressing plays a large role in the piecing process. There is an endless debate over whether it is better to press seams to one side or open. No matter which you decide to do, someone will disagree. I suggest that you try both and find which you prefer. When I started quilting, I pressed to one side, but I am now a pressing-open convert. Both techniques have their pros and cons. It's easier to press to one side, but I like how flat all of the piecing lies when I press open.

Pressing is not the same thing as ironing. You should press down, lift your iron, and press it down again, working your way along the seam to avoid distorting the fabric. If you just slide the iron along your fabric with pressure, you might distort it and your piecing.

I first press along the wrong side of the piecing, sometimes using a bit of steam if needed. Then I flip the piecing over and press again on the front of the piecing.

Making the Quilt Backing

The backing should be about 5″ bigger than your quilt top on all sides. This gives you extra fabric to center the top on, as well as extra fabric to hold on to so you can quilt to the very edge of the quilt top.

If you plan to send your quilt to a longarm quilter (see Longarm Quilting, page 138), check with the quilter to determine how big the quilt back needs to be. Longarm quilters often need the back to be a specific size so that it loads correctly onto the rack.

Batting

Batting is the layer of filling that goes between the quilt top and quilt back, giving the quilt its wonderful drape and weight. There is a huge variety of battings on the market—everything from 100% polyester to 100% organic cotton. There are also battings made of silk, wool, bamboo, and recycled plastic bottles. All of these different battings have different lofts (the height and puffiness of the batting), and they all breathe differently. I use Warm and Natural batting (by The Warm Company), a low-loft, mostly cotton batting that I love. It breathes wonderfully and has a great drape. On principle, I tend to stay away from polyester battings, but if you are after the look, they can create a very puffy quilt. Wool and silk battings can be wonderful too, but the prices can be high. Try different battings and see which ones you like best.

Making the Quilt Sandwich

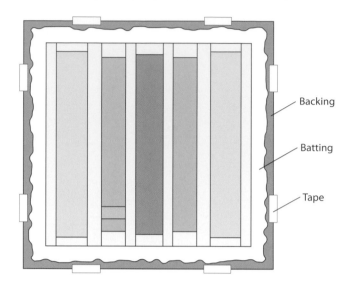

Backing

Batting

Tape

Note

If you spray baste your quilt, layer at the same time that you baste. If you pin baste, layer first and then baste.

The next step in making a quilt is to layer all three parts of the quilt: the quilt top, the batting, and the back.

The bigger the quilt, the more time consuming this step is. If your quilt is small enough to layer on a table, then do so. If it is bigger, you have to do it on the floor. A hard, smooth floor is key—hardwood, tile, or linoleum. Avoid rugs or carpet because these floor coverings make it difficult to get the quilt back smooth and flat.

1. Make sure the floor is clean. I'll admit that my kitchen floor is only mopped when I need to baste a quilt. Good thing that's frequently!

2. Tape down the quilt back, wrong side up, so it lies nice and flat but isn't pulled too tightly. You don't want any of it to become distorted.

3. Carefully layer the batting and the quilt top on top of the quilt back. This step can be tiresome and takes some crawling around on the floor. But be sure to take your time to center the quilt top on the quilt back and to smooth out any bumps or lumps in the layers.

Basting

Once the quilt sandwich is layered, it's time to baste it together to prevent the layers from shifting as you quilt them.

There are different ways to baste the layers of a quilt sandwich.

- *Spray basting with spray-on basting glue:*
  Spray basting can be messy, so do it outside and follow the directions on the can.

- *Sewing large stitches through the layers:*
  Be sure to use contrasting thread, so the stitches are easy to see and pull out later.

- *Pin basting:*
  This is exactly what it sounds like—using safety pins to baste the quilt.

Pin basting is my preferred method, and the way demonstrated in the following instructions. This step can be tedious, but being thorough is the key to keeping the layers together well while you quilt. You don't want the layers slip-sliding around and shifting. This can lead to puckers on the quilt back—something I struggled with when I made my first few quilts. Once I started to pin baste more thoroughly, however, this problem disappeared completely.

To pin baste, work your way around the quilt face, pinning through all three layers. I pin every 4"–5" in a grid pattern.

If you know where your quilting lines will fall, avoid those areas with the pins, if possible.

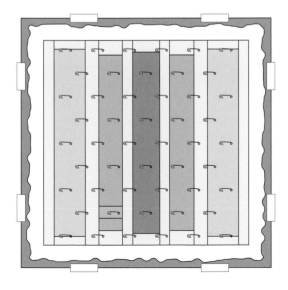

Quilting

Quilting means two things: It is both the entire process of making a quilt and the step in which the quilter sews through the quilt sandwich. This latter step is what makes a quilt a quilt and not just a bed cover. It adds so much to the beauty of a quilt—texture, depth, and interest.

When I was learning to make quilts, I found that in the tons and tons of information about modern quiltmaking, the one step that is discussed the least is stitching the quilting. There is a huge focus on making the quilt top. And yet stitching the quilting is so important and plays an equally large role in the finished look of a quilt.

Many people are daunted by the idea and task of quilting a big quilt on their home sewing machine, but it can be done. I quilted all the quilts in this book on my machine. Granted, I have a Janome Horizon, a nice big sewing machine that has a very large harp (the open space in the middle of the machine through which you have to squeeze the quilt); but in the past, I quilted more than one king-sized quilt on my first, and very basic, sewing machine.

People also often worry that they will "ruin" their quilt top with quilting. I find that no matter how simple or basic the quilting, it always makes a quilt top even prettier. Someone once said to me, "The best kind of quilt is a finished one," and I took that to heart. I personally think that a quilt that is finished, even with quilting you aren't in love with, is so much better than a random quilt top sitting in a sewing cupboard. Some people make one quilt top after another and never finish them. I'll admit that this is a pet peeve of mine, as I think it's like mixing up batter and never baking the cake. Don't you want to be cozy under the quilt on your couch? If you finish it, you can enjoy it for years to come!

I have learned all I know about quilting simply by doing it and doing it a lot. There is one overriding and most important tip to quilting: *Practice!*

Straight-Line Quilting

Straight-line quilting is exactly what it sounds like—sewing straight lines through the quilt sandwich. Countless patterns and designs can be produced with this method.

Dense vertical lines (see *Art Deco*, page 40)

To straight-line quilt, you need a walking foot for your sewing machine. This foot has feed dogs that help to evenly feed all the layers of a quilt sandwich though the machine.

I increase my stitch length when I am straight-line quilting. This makes the stitches bigger, a look I like. Since the stitches provide texture but are not structurally holding together two pieces of fabric, it's perfectly fine to make them big.

Diagonal allover pattern (see *Mosaic*, page 68)   Big straight-line spiral (see *Hot Spot*, page 96)

Free-Motion Quilting

Free-motion quilting is like drawing on your quilt, only you are moving the paper and not the pen. The single biggest tip for free-motion quilting on a home sewing machine is to do it a lot. The more you practice, the more you'll learn the ins and outs of your machine, and the smoother your quilting will become. With time, you'll learn whether your machine sews one last stitch once you take your foot off the pedal. You'll soon know your sewing machine the way you know your car. Don't be scared—start on something small and give it a shot. Make pot holders and place mats until you're ready for something bigger, and then dive into a baby quilt. With some practice, you'll be comfortable with free-motion quilting in no time.

To free-motion quilt, you need a darning foot (also sometimes called a *free-motion foot*) for your machine. You also need to lower the feed dogs. If the feed dogs do not lower, check the manual, because you may be able to cover them.

If you have the feature on your machine, set your needle to stop in the down position so you can stop and start as much as you need to without your quilt moving around. If your machine doesn't have this feature, just always remember to roll your needle into the down position when you want to pause to rearrange your quilt.

When you free-motion quilt, the stitch length is determined by the speed at which you move your hands, in relation to the pressure you apply to the foot pedal. If you move the fabric quickly, you will create large stitches, whereas moving slowly will create small stitches, unless you adjust the speed of the needle to compensate. Plan to move your hands steadily and at a medium pace. The key to free-motion quilting is to find the right balance between the speed the needle moves and the speed you move your quilt.

Some machines require different tension settings when free-motion quilting, so sew a test pattern on a scrap sandwich before you start on your quilt top. A test will let you check that your machine's tension is correct. If it is not, try adjusting it to find out which setting gives you the best stitches. I find that my machine's tension usually needs to be adjusted up for free-motion quilting, but it really does vary from machine to machine.

Plan how you will work through your quilt before you start quilting. You always want to have as little of the quilt in the throat of the machine as possible. It's not always easy to squeeze a big quilt through a little machine, but it can be done!

If the bobbin runs out of thread in the middle of the quilt, replace the bobbin, trimming any loose threads, and keep going from the same spot, making sure to sew a few locking stitches over where you left off.

> **TIP**
>
> When quilting a large quilt, it helps to have tables both behind and to the left of your sewing machine to hold some of the quilt's weight. An extension table, if available for your machine, is also hugely helpful in maneuvering a large quilt.

One last thing to keep in mind with free-motion quilting is that the big picture is much more important than each square inch you quilt. If you make the occasional small flaw as you quilt, remember that you'll never see it when you step back and look at the quilt as a whole.

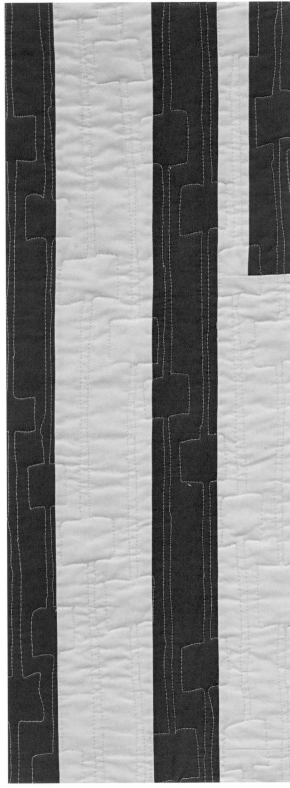

Boxy mod pattern (see *Drip*, page 8)

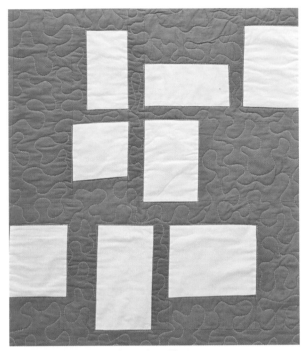

Allover stippling or meandering (see *Cluster*, page 73

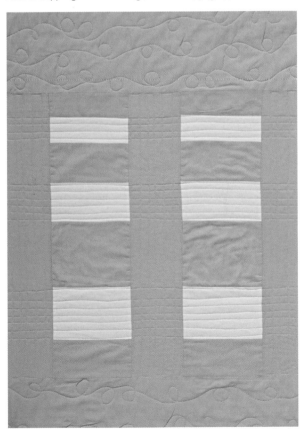

Cute curlicues (see *Don't Fence Me In*, page 108)

Longarm Quilting

Longarm quilting is when the quilter quilts on a longarm quilting machine. With this setup, the quilt is loaded on a rack, and the needle moves over the quilt surface. It's like proper drawing, moving the pen over the paper, as opposed to quilting on a domestic machine, which is the opposite. The freedom that this process provides allows for amazing quilting patterns and intricate details that most quilters find difficult to produce on their home machines. However, the cost of these machines is out of range for most quilters.

You might be able to take a class and rent time on a longarm machine at your local quilt shop. There are also many professional longarm quilters who can quilt your top for a fee.

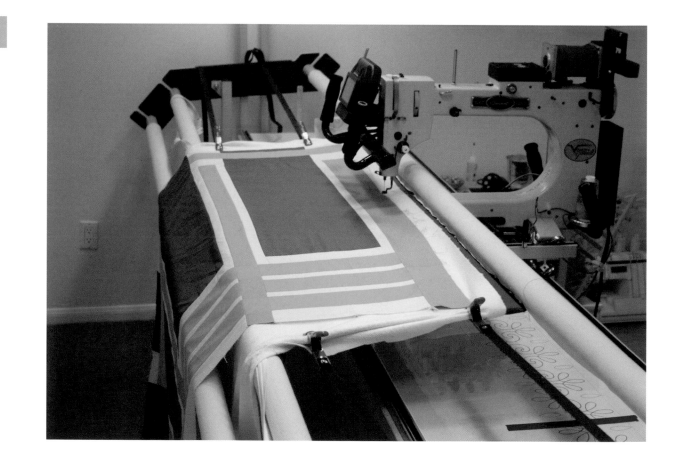

Hand Quilting

Hand quilting is an age-old tradition that leads to astonishingly beautiful results. That said, I'll admit to never having hand quilted a quilt. It is very, very time consuming, and many people find they want to get their quilts finished faster than hand quilting allows. If you enjoy hand stitching, maybe hand quilting is for you. Or perhaps you have a special quilt that you want to put hours of your handwork into. If you hand quilt a quilt, you'll create a priceless heirloom that will stay with a family for generations.

To hand quilt, you need a needle (choose a short, sharp needle with an eye large enough for the thread); some cotton quilting thread, perle cotton, or embroidery thread; a thimble; and a quilting frame or hoop.

Choose a quilting design. If necessary, mark the design on your quilt. Start by placing the center of the quilt in a hoop or frame, centering the portion you wish to quilt. Thread your needle with about 18"–24" of thread. Knot one end of the thread. Working from the top, insert the needle down through the first layer, through the batting and

then back to the surface. Give the thread a firm tug to pull the knot through the quilt top, burying it in the batting.

With a thimble on the middle or index finger of your dominant hand, whatever is comfortable, sew a small running stitch along the determined quilting design. Holding the quilt underneath with your other hand, use the thimble to rock the needle back and forth, going through the three layers of the quilt sandwich and making small stitches.

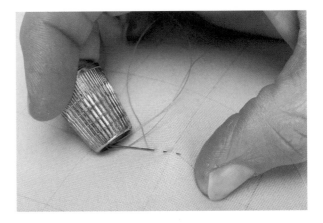

Once your thread is too short to keep quilting, tie another knot and bury it in the quilt sandwich.

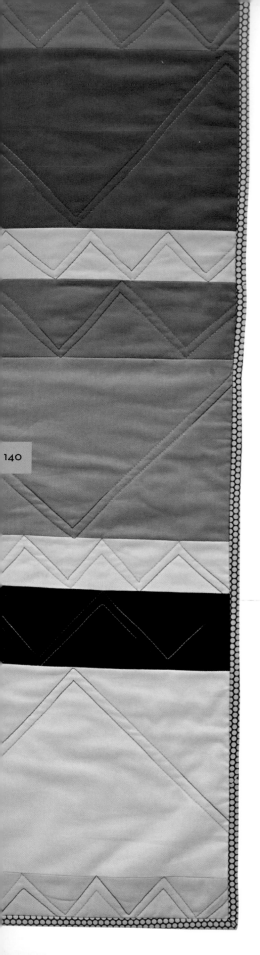

Binding

Binding adds the finished edge to a quilt. There is such satisfaction in putting on the binding. It means the quilt is almost finished! I like to use 3/8" finished binding.

Use a rotary cutter, ruler, and mat to square up your quilt, trimming off the excess batting and backing fabric 1/8" beyond the edge of the quilt top.

Making Binding

First, you must do some math to figure out the binding length. Yes, math. I'm sorry. But there's not too much of it, and it's simple.

To figure out how many inches of binding you need, add up the length of all four sides of the quilt. *For example:*

> If your quilt is 60" × 70", then you need
> 60" + 60" + 70" + 70" = 260" of binding.

> To ensure that I never make too little binding, I then add 15" more to that number.

> I cut my binding strips 2½" wide. Because we know that quilting cottons measure at least 40" from selvage to selvage (WOF), you can use that number to calculate how many 2½" × WOF strips you'll need to cut.

> For our example, 275" ÷ 40" = 6.875. Round up to cut 7 strips 2½" wide.

> If you need 7 or more strips, add 1 extra strip. This will make up for the fabric lost to the diagonal seams used to piece the strips together.

Apply this math to any quilt to work out how many inches of binding you need and how many 2½" × WOF strips you'll need to cut to make that many inches.

Straight-Grain Binding

1. Cut as many 2½″ × WOF (width of fabric, selvage to selvage) strips as you need.

2. Piece together the strips end to end, using diagonal seams to distribute the bulk of the folded seams.

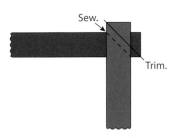

3. Trim the diagonal seams to ¼″ seam allowances and press open.

4. Press the strips in half, wrong sides together, along the entire length of the binding.

Attaching Binding

1. Leaving a 12″ tail loose and starting about halfway down an edge of the quilt, line up the raw edges of the binding with the raw edge of the quilt front. Some people like to pin the binding in place at this point, but you don't have to. Begin stitching.

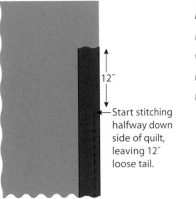

12″

Start stitching halfway down side of quilt, leaving 12″ loose tail.

Note

I use a ⅜″ seam allowance when attaching binding, as it gives more quilt to wrap the binding around.

2. Stop stitching ⅜″ from the corner and backstitch. Take the quilt out of the machine.

Stop stitching ⅜″ from edge of quilt top.

3. To create a mitered corner, fold the binding to the right at a right angle, making sure that the bottom of the quilt and the bottom edge of the binding line up in a straight line.

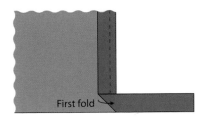

First fold

4. Fold the binding straight back to the left.

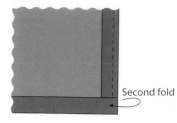

Second fold

5. Turn the quilt a quarter-turn and continue sewing down the binding.

6. Work your way around all 4 corners of the quilt. Once you turn the fourth corner, continue until you are about 18″ from where you started. Make sure you leave a loose tail on this end as well.

7. Trim the 2 loose ends, so that they overlap by 2½″.

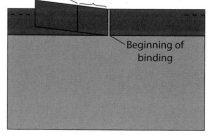

Cut.   Overlap 2 loose ends by 2½″.

Beginning of binding

8. Open and position the ends right sides together, as shown. Pin in place and sew the ends together with a diagonal seam.

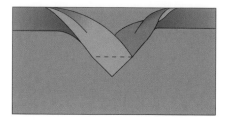

9. Trim the seam allowance to ¼″ and press the seam open.

10. Sew the remainder of the binding down to the quilt face.

11. Fold the binding to the back of the quilt and hand stitch using a blind stitch with matching thread. With each stitch, take care not to push the needle through to the front of the quilt (so that your stitches don't show on the front), but move it through the quilt back and batting layers.

Note

With a large quilt, hand stitching a binding can be time consuming, but I am a traditionalist about hand stitching bindings (it's the only thing in quilting that I feel this way about!). I don't think you can replicate the wonderful finished look with any method of machine stitching. That said, if you know yourself, and you won't finish your quilt because of the hand stitching, by all means Google "machine binding techniques" and learn one of the many that exist!

Now let's apply all this info to the 20 projects in the book! Let's make some quilts!

142

ABOUT THE AUTHOR

ALISSA HAIGHT CARLTON lives in Los Angeles with her filmmaker husband. She is one of the founders of the Modern Quilt Guild. Her work has been published in *Stitch* magazine, *Quilter's Home*, and Quilting Arts' *Quilt Scene*. When not quilting, she casts reality shows, including seasons seven, eight, and nine of *Project Runway*. Alissa blogs about her quilting at handmadebyalissa.com.

143

Other favorite modern quilting blogs and online sources:

Jacquie Gering
tallgrassprairiestudio.blogspot.com

Elizabeth Hartman
ohfransson.com

Ashley Newcomb
filminthefridge.com

Community online
Fresh Modern Quilts
flickr.com/groups/freshmodernquilts

Community in person
The Modern Quilt Guild
themodernquiltguild.com

Also by Alissa Haight Carlton:

Also available as an eBook